Marlon Brando

Portraits and Film Stills
1946-1995

Marlon Brando

Portraits and Film Stills
1946-1995

With an essay by
Truman Capote

Edited by Lothar Schirmer

STEWART, TABORI AND CHANG

NEW YORK

Published in 1996 and distributed in the U.S. by Stewart, Tabori & Chang, a division of U.S. Media Holdings, Inc. 575 Broadway, New York, New York 10012 Distributed in Canada by General Publishing Co. Ltd. 30 Lesmill Road, Don Mills, Ontario, Canada M3B T6

ISBN: 1-55670-463-1

Library of Congress Card Catalog Number: 95-072884

10 9 8 7 6 5 4 3 2 1

First Edition
Printed in Germany

A Schirmer/Mosel Production

Contents

Preface

The idea of producing a book of photos of Marlon Brando came to me for the first time once while I was doing my usual round of window-shopping through all the TV channels, and my attention was suddenly caught by a film in which Francis Ford Coppola's wife had recorded the shooting of *Apocalypse Now* in the Philippines.

Even Marlon Brando's arrival on location was extraordinary. And then, as if falling into a trance, he started saying his first words as Major Kurtz. An alarming, terrifying metamorphosis of his whole personality took place, and I felt a shiver go down my spine. It was as if the *Heart of Darkness* had actually started to beat. A witch doctor conjuring up spirits could not have been more impressive.

What finally stimulated me to go on and actually do something about the idea was the TV once again. A few months ago, Austrian television showed a documentary about Brando (which the station produced itself, if my memory serves me correctly). The program included an interview with a very private, seventy-year-old Brando, whose sumo-wrestling figure had blown his jeans up into the shape of a hammock. His whole colossal weight, however, was canceled out by the liveliest face and the most glittering eyes imaginable. On top of this, he had a relaxed sense of humor and an effervescent sense of enjoying life that is rarely found even in younger people, and is almost never seen in TV programs about important people.

The physical impression that Brando's appearance made on me was so strong that the very next day I set about doing what had till then just been a vague notion. I wrote to all the photo archives, picture agencies, and photographers I thought might possibly have pictures of Brando. Over the following six weeks, a whole flood of pictorial material poured across my desk, and there seemed to be no end to it. Then, with two of my staff, I spent a couple of days selecting the three hundred most impressive pictures from the thousands we had. On the third day, we sifted out of this again the ones that are reproduced in this book. By this time, we were all as exhausted as if we had just spent three days walking through the British Museum.

We left this first draft of the plates aside for three weeks, to recover our strength and get a bit of perspective on the material. During this time, I started thinking about what kind of text might help to give the book the extra literary quality it needed.

Of course, there was only one person capable of writing the biography, captions, and insert texts—our editor Daniel Dreier, who has been in charge of our "diva" series (the in-house slang for all the company's books about actors) since the very start.

It was more difficult to choose a source for the introductory essay. Marlon Brando's autobiography, published in 1994 under the title *Brando: Songs My Mother Taught Me,* would certainly have provided an authentic and almost unrivaled source. But of course, Brando's autobiography suffers from two of the well-known weaknesses of the genre. First, like most autobiographies, it is only really interesting up to the point at which the author has become the person who was asked to write the autobiography—a point that actually occurs quite early in Brando's life, even before his thirtieth birthday. Secondly, the accuracy of autobiographical writing can usually only be assessed using psychological methods; and this problem is obviously raised to an even higher scale when we are dealing with the autobiographical writings of an actor—and an actor who is one of the most outstanding members of his profession. To borrow the elegant formulation used by Harold Brodkey when he reviewed the book in the *New Yorker,* "But let's call it a lie, for it is clearly a performance. ... Brando is an actor and has lied for a living all of his life—lied and presented a simulacrum of truth." And, later on, "His autobiography is intelligent, and, as I said, the more he lies the more a sense of truth emerges."

Brando would not be Brando if he had not long since made himself immune, both in his ego and in his work, to all sorts of objections—by anticipating them with his own self-criticism. For example, by quite casually describing his own book as "trash": "I'm writing this book for money because Harry Evans of Random House offered it to me. He said that if his company published a book about a movie

star, the profits would enable him to publish books by talented unpublished authors that might not make money. At least he was honest, although I thought it was odd for him to admit that he published trashy books so that he could issue those that had real value." One has the utmost sympathy for poor Harry, who had to pay an advance of five million dollars for this "trash!" Or again, when Brando casually wonders what he might have been if he hadn't been an actor: "I think I'd have made a good con man; I'm good at telling lies smoothly, giving an impression of things as they are not and making people think I'm sincere. A good con man can fool anybody, but the first person he fools is himself." So, let readers beware—and if they are fooled nevertheless, they have scant reason to complain, since they are in good company here with the author.

But if Brando's book is a piece of self-dramatization, as Brodkey observes, one might well ask what the script is. I found the answer in Truman Capote's literary portrait of Brando—written in 1956, when Brando, at the peak of his first world hits, was shooting *Sayonara* in Japan. When Capote published the text in the *New Yorker* in 1957, Brando was so furious that he stopped giving interviews for years afterwards. Truman Capote—born, like Brando, in 1924—refers to the incident in the introduction to his collection of essays, *The Dog's Bark:* "Of all my sitters, the one most distressed was the subject of *The Duke in His Domain,* Marlon Brando. Though not claiming any inaccuracy, he apparently felt it was an unsympathetic, even treacherous intrusion upon the secret terrain of a suffering and intellectually awesome sensibility. My opinion? Just that it is a pretty good account, and a sympathetic one, of a wounded young man who is a genius, but *not* markedly intelligent."

When one compares the piece by Capote with

Brando's autobiography, it seems that in his own book, Brando, while not entirely living up to Capote's psychological characterization in certain points, nowhere goes beyond it. To this extent, Capote's portrait has remained, alongside the autobiography, *the* ultimate text on Brando—although it should be noted that Capote's mocking and critical reservations about the young acting genius's philanthropic ambitions have in the meantime been refuted by Brando's actual life. The fact that Brando does not mention Truman Capote anywhere in his autobiography, almost forty years on, is in itself an indication that this hypothesis is correct, and that Brando at best reveals himself in his own book to precisely the same extent that he had already been revealed by Capote. With the brilliance of the style and substance of Truman Capote's text, in spite of its date, it therefore seemed to me that it was very suitable as the introductory essay for this book. It accurately and sympathetically reflects the difficult psychological position of a heroic figure who is in the extreme situation of being a supposed outcast, on the one hand, and an obvious King Midas, on the other.

Two more decisions still had to be made. First, which picture of Brando to use for the cover. In the company, opinion was divided. There was a group of biker fans who preferred a still from *The Wild One,* and there was a Tahiti faction. As you can see, it was the biker faction that won.

And finally, the plate section had to be given finishing touches in order to "synchronize" the text with the pictures.

One of the outstanding figures of the century can now be viewed in all his glory.

Lothar Schirmer

The Duke in His Domain

Most Japanese girls giggle. The little maid on the fourth floor of the Miyako Hotel, in Kyoto, was no exception. Hilarity, and attempts to suppress it, pinked her cheeks (unlike the Chinese, the Japanese complexion more often than not has considerable color), shook her plump peony-and-pansy-kimonoed figure. There seemed to be no particular reason for this merriment; the Japanese giggle operates without apparent motivation. I'd merely asked to be directed toward a certain room. "You come see Marron?" she gasped, showing, like so many of her fellow-countrymen, an array of gold teeth. Then, with the tiny, pigeon-toed skating steps that the wearing of a kimono necessitates, she led me through a labyrinth of corridors, promising, "I knock you Marron." The "L" sound does not exist in Japanese, and by "Marron" the maid meant Marlon—Marlon Brando, the American actor, who was at that time in Kyoto doing location work for the Warner Brothers-William Goetz motion-picture version of James Michener's novel *Sayonara.*

My guide tapped at Brando's door, shrieked "Marron!" and fled away along the corridor, her kimono sleeves fluttering like the wings of a parakeet. The door was opened by another doll-delicate Miyako maid, who at once succumbed to her own fit of quaint hysteria. From an inner room, Brando called, "What is it, honey?" But the girl, her eyes squeezed shut with mirth and her fat little hands jammed into her mouth, like a bawling baby's, was incapable of reply. "Hey, honey, what is it?" Brando again inquired, and appeared in the doorway. "Oh, hi," he said when he saw me. "It's seven, huh?" We'd made a seven-o'clock date for dinner; I was nearly twenty minutes late. "Well, take off your shoes and come on in. I'm just finishing up here. And, hey, honey," he told the maid, "bring us some ice." Then, looking after the girl as she scurried off, he cocked his hands on his hips and, grinning, declared, "They kill me. They really kill me. The kids, too. Don't you think they're wonderful, don't you love them—Japanese kids?"

The Miyako, where about half of the "Sayonara" company was staying, is the most prominent of the so-called Western-style hotels in Kyoto; the majority of its rooms are furnished with sturdy, if commonplace and cumbersome, European chairs and tables, beds and couches. But, for the convenience of Japanese guests who prefer their own mode of décor while desiring the prestige of staying at the Miyako, or of those foreign travelers who yearn after authentic atmosphere yet are disinclined to endure the unheated rigors of a real Japanese inn, in Miyako maintains some suites decorated in the traditional manner, and it was in one of these that Brando had chosen to settle himself. His quarters consisted of two rooms, a bath, and a glassed-in sun porch. Without the overlying and underlying clutter of Brando's personal belongings, the rooms would have been textbook illustrations of the Japanese penchant for an ostentatious barrenness. The floors were covered with tawny *tatami* matting, with a discreet scattering of raw-silk pillows; a scroll depicting swimming golden carp hung in an alcove, and beneath it, on a stand, sat a vase filled with tall lilies and red leaves, arranged just so. The larger of the two rooms—the inner one—which the occupant was using as a sort of business office where he also dined and slept, contained a long, low lacquer table and a sleeping pallet. In these rooms, the divergent concepts of Japanese and Western decoration—the one seeking to impress by a lack of display, an absence of possession-exhibiting, the other intent on precisely the reverse—could both be observed, for Brando seemed unwilling to make use of the apartment's storage space, concealed behind sliding paper door. All that he owned seemed to be out in the open. Shirts, ready for the laundry; socks, too; shoes and sweaters and jackets and hats and ties, flung around like the costume of a dismantled scarecrow. And cameras, a typewriter, a tape recorder, an electric heater that performed with stifling competence. Here, there, pieces of partly nibbled fruit; a box of the famous Japanese strawberries, each berry the size of an egg. And books, a deep-thought cascade, among which one saw Colin Wilson's *The Outsider* and various works on Buddhist prayer, Zen meditation, Yogi breathing, and Hindu mysticism, but no fiction, for Brando

reads none. He has never, he professes, opened a novel since April 3, 1924, the day he was born, in Omaha, Nebraska. But while he may not care to read fiction, he does desire to write it, and the long lacquer table was loaded with overfilled ash trays and piled pages of his most recent creative effort, which happens to be a film script entiled *A Burst of Vermilion*.

In fact, Brando had evidently been working on his story at the moment of my arrival. As I entered the room, a subdued-looking, youngish man, whom I shall call Murray, and who had previously been pointed out to me as "the fellow that's helping Marlon with his writing," was squatted on the matting fumbling through the manuscript of *A Burst of Vermilion*. Weighing some pages on his hand, he said, "Tell ya, Mar, s'pose I go over this down in my room, and maybe we'll get together again—say, around ten-thirty?"

Brando scowled, as though unsympathetic to the idea of resuming their endeavors later in the evening. Having been slightly ill, as I learned later, he had spent the day in his room, and now seemed restive. "What's this?" he asked, pointing to a couple of oblong packages among the literary remains on the lacquer table.

Murray shrugged. The maid had delivered them; that was all he knew. "People are always sending Mar presents," he told me. "Lots of times we don't know who sent them. True, Mar?"

"Yeah," said Brando, beginning to rip open the gifts, which, like most Japanese packages—even mundane purchases from very ordinary shops—were beautifully wrapped. One contained candy, the other white rice cakes, which proved cement-hard, though they looked like puffs of cloud. There was no card in either package to identify the donor. "Every time you turn around, some Japanese is giving you a present. They're crazy about giving presents,"

Brando observed. Athletically crunching a rice cake, he passed the boxes to Murray and me.

Murray shook his head; he was intent on obtaining Brando's promise to meet with him again at ten-thirty. "Give me a ring around then," Brando said, finally. "We'll see what's happening."

Murray, as I knew, was only one member of what some of the *Sayonara* company referred to as "Brando's gang." Aside form the literary assistant, the gang consisted of Marlon Brando, Sr., who acts as his son's business manager; a pretty, dark-haired secretary, Miss Levin; and Brando's private makeup man. The travel expenses of this entourage, and all its living expenses while on location, were allowed for in the actor's contract with Warner Brothers. Legend to the contrary, film studios are not usually so lenient financially. A Warner man to whom I talked later explained the tolerance shown Brando by saying, "Ordinarily we wouldn't put up with it. All the demands he makes. Except—well, this picture just *had* to have a big star. Your star—that's the only thing that really counts at the box office."

Among the company were some who felt that the social protection supplied by Brando's inner circle was preventing them from "getting to know the guy" as well as they would have liked. Brando had been in Japan for more than a month, and during that time he had shown himself on the set a slouchingly dignified, amiable-seeming young man who was always ready to co-operate with, and even encourage, his co-workers—the actors particularly—yet by and large was not socially available, preferring, during the tedious lulls between scenes, to sit alone reading philosophy or scribbling in a schoolboy notebook. After the day's work, instead of accepting his colleagues' invitations to join a group for drinks, a plate of raw fish in a restaurant, and a prowl though the old geisha quarter of Kyoto, instead of contributing to the one-big-family,

houseparty bonhomie that picture-making on location theoretically generates, he usually returned to his hotel and stayed there. Since the most fervent of movie-star fans are the people who themselves work in the film industry, Brando was a subject of immense interest within the ranks of the *Sayonara* group, and the more so because his attitude of friendly remoteness produced, in the face of such curiosity, such wistful frustrations. Even the film's director, Joshua Logan, was impelled to say, after working with Brando for two weeks, "Marlon's the most exciting person I've met since Garbo. A genius. But I don't know what he's like. I don't know anything about him."

The maid had re-entered the star's room, and Murray, on his way out, almost tripped over the train of her kimono. She put down a bowl of ice and, with a glow,
a giggle, an elation that made her little feet, hooflike in their split-toed white socks, lift and lower like a prancing pony's, announced, "Appapie! Tonight on menu appapie."

Brando groaned. "Apple pie. That's all I need." He stretched out on the floor and unbuckled his belt, which dug too deeply into the swell of his stomach. "I'm supposed to be on a diet. But the only things I want to eat are apple pie and stuff like that." Six weeks earlier, in California, Logan had told him he must trim off ten pounds for his role in *Sayonara,* and before arriving in Kyoto he had managed to get rid of seven. Since reaching Japan, however, abetted not only by American-type apple pie but by the Japanese cuisine, with its delicious emphasis on the sweetened, the starchy, the fried, he'd regained, then doubled this poundage. Now, loosening his belt still more and thoughtfully massaging his midriff, he scanned the menu, which offered, in English, a wide choice of Western-style dishes, and, after reminding himself "I've *got* to lose weight," he ordered soup, beefsteak with French-fried potatoes, three supplementary vegetables, a side dish of spaghetti, rolls and butter, a bottle of *sake*, salad, and cheese and crackers.

"And appapie, Marron?"

He sighed. "With ice cream, honey."

Though Brando is not a teetotaller, his appetite is more frugal when it comes to alcohol. While we were awaiting the dinner, which was to be served to us in the room, he supplied me with a large vodka on the rocks and poured himself the merest courtesy sip. Resuming his position on the floor, he lolled his head against a pillow, dropped his eyelids, then shut them. It was as though he'd dozed off into a disturbing dream; his eyelids twitched, and when he spoke, his voice—an unemotional voice, in a way cultivated and genteel, yet surprisingly adolescent, a voice with a probing, asking, boyish quality—seemed to come from sleepy distances.

"The last eight, nine years of my life have been a mess," he said. "Maybe the last two have been a little better. Less rolling in the trough of the wave. Have you ever been analyzed? I was afraid of it at first. Afraid it might destroy the impulse that made me creative, an artist. A sensitive person receives fifty impressions where somebody else may only get seven. Sensitive people are so vulnerable; they're so easily brutalized and hurt just because they *are* sensitive. The more sensitive you are, the more certain you are to be brutalized, develop scabs. Never evolve. Never allow yourself to feel anything, because you always feel too much. Analysis helps. It helped me. But still, the last eight, nine years I've been pretty mixed up, a mess pretty much...."

The voice went on, as though speaking to hear itself, an effect Brando's speech often has, for, like many persons who are intensely self-absorbed, he is something of a monologuist—a fact that he recognizes and for which he offers his own explanation.

"People around me never say anything," he says. "They just seem to want to hear what I have to say. That's why I do all the talking." Watching him now, with his eyes closed, his unlined face white under an overhead light, I felt as if the moment of my initial encounter with him were being recreated. The year of that meeting was 1947; it was a winter afternoon in New York, when I had occasion to attend a rehearsal of Tennessee Williams' *A Streetcar Named Desire*, in which Brando was to play the role of Stanley Kowalski. It was this role that first brought him general recognition, although among the New York theatre's cognoscenti he had already attracted attention, through his student work with the drama coach Stella Adler and a few Broadway appearances—one in a play by Maxwell Anderson, *Truckline Café*, and another as Marchbanks opposite Katharine Cornell's Candida—in which he showed an ability that had been much praised and discussed. Elia Kazan, the director of *A Streetcar Named Desire*, said at that time, and has recently repeated, "Marlon is just the best actor in the world." But ten years ago, on the remembered afternoon, he was still relatively unknown; at least, I hadn't a clue to who he might be when, arriving too early at the *Streetcar* rehearsal, I found the auditorium deserted and a brawny young man stretched out atop a table on the stage under the gloomy glare of work lights, solidly asleep. Because he was wearing a white T shirt and denim trousers, because of his squat gymnasium physique—the weight-lifter's arms, the Charles Atlas chest (though an opened *Basic Writings of Sigmund Freud* was resting on it)—I took him for a stagehand. Or did until I looked closely at his face. It was as if a stranger's head had been attached to the brawny body, as in certain counterfeit photographs. For this face was so very untough, superimposing, as it did, an almost angelic refinement and gentleness upon hard-jawed good looks: taut skin, a broad, high forehead, wide-apart eyes, an aqualine nose, full lips with a relaxed, sensual expression. Not the least suggestion of Williams' unpoetic Kowalski. It was therefore rather an experience to observe, later that afternoon, with what chameleon ease Brando acquired the character's cruel and gaudy colors, how superbly, like a guileful salamander, he slithered into the part, how his own persona evaporated—just as, in this Kyoto hotel room ten years afterward, my 1947 memory of Brando receded, disappeared into his 1957 self. And the present Brando, the one lounging there on the *tatami* and lazily puffing filtered cigarettes as he talked and talked, was, of course, a different person—bound to be. His body was thicker; his forehead was higher, for his hair was thinner; he was richer (from the producers of *Sayonara* he could expect a salary of three hundred thousand dollars, plus a percentage of the picture's earnings); and he'd become, as one journalist put it, "the Valentino of the bop generation"—turned into such a world celebrity that when he went out in public here in Japan, he deemed it wise to hide his face not only by wearing dark glasses but by donning a surgeon's gauze mask as well. (The latter bit of disguise is not so *outré* in Japan as is may sound, since numerous Asians wear such masks, on the theory that they prevent the spreading of germs.) Those were some of the alterations a decade had made. There were others. His eyes had changed. Although their *café-espresso* color was the same, the shyness, any traces of real vulnerability that they had formerly held, had left them; now he looked at people with assurance, and with what can only be called a pitying expression, as though he dwelt in spheres of enlightenment where they, to his regret, did not. (The reactions of the people subjected to this gaze of constant commiseration range from that of a young actress who avowed that "Marlon is really a very *spiritual* person, wise and very sincere;

you can see it in his eyes" to that of a Brando acquaintance who said, "The way he looks at you, like he was so damm sorry for you—doesn't it make you want to cut your throat?") Nevertheless, the subtly tender character of his face had been preserved. Or almost. For in the years between he'd had an accident that gave his face a more conventionally masculine aspect. It was just that his nose had been broken. And, maneuvering a word in edgewise, I asked, "How did you break your nose?"

"... by which I don't mean that I'm *always* unhappy. I remember one April I was in Sicily. A hot day, and flowers everywhere. I like flowers, the ones that smell. Gardenias. Anyway, it was April and I was in Sicily, and I went off by myself. Lay down in this field of flowers. Went to sleep. That made me happy. I was happy *then*. What? You say something?"

"I was wondering how you broke your nose."

He rubbed his nose and grinned, as though remembering an experience as happy as the Sicilian nap. "That was a long time ago. I did it boxing. It was when I was in *Streetcar*. We, some of the guys backstage and me—we used to go down to the boiler room in the theatre and horse around, mix it up. One night, I was mixing it up with this guy and—crack! So I put on my coat and walked around to the nearest hospital—it was off Broadway somewhere. My nose was really busted. They had to give me an anesthetic to set it, and put me to bed. Not that I was sorry. *Streetcar* had been running about a year and I was sick of it. But my nose healed pretty quick, and I guess I would've been back in the show practically right away if I hadn't done what I did to Irene Selznick." His grin broadened as he mentioned Mrs. Selznick, who had been the producer of the Williams play. "There is one shrewd lady, Irene Selznick. When she wants something, she wants it. And she wanted me back in the play. But when I heard she was coming to the hospital, I went to work with bandages and iodine and mercurochrome, and—Christ!—when she walked in the door, I looked like my head had been cut off. At the least. And *sounded* as though I were dying. 'Oh, Marlon,' she said 'you poor, *poor* boy!' And I said, 'Don't you worry about anything, Irene. I'll be back in the show tonight!' And she said, 'Don't you dare! We can manage without you for—for—well, a *few* days more.' 'No, no,' I said. 'I'm O.K. I want to work. Tell them I'll be back tonight.' So she said, 'You're in no condition, you poor darling. I *forbid* you to come to the theatre.' So I stayed in the hospital and had myself a ball." (Mrs. Selznick, recalling the incident recently, said, "They didn't set his nose properly at all. Suddenly his face was quite different. Kind of tough. For months afterward, I kept telling him, 'But they've *ruined* your face. You must have your nose broken again and reset.' Luckily for him, he didn't listen to me. Because I honestly think that broken nose made his fortune as far as the movies go. It gave him sex appeal. He was too beautiful before.")

Brando made his first trip to the Coast in 1949, when he went out there to play the leading role in *The Men,* a picture dealing with paraplegic war veterans. He was accused, at the time, of uncouth social conduct, and criticized for his black-leather-jacket taste in attire, his choice of motorcycles instead of Jaguars, and his preference for obscure secretaries rather than movie starlets; moreover, Hollywood columnists studded their copy with hostile comments concerning his attitude toward the film business, which he himself summed up soon after he entered it by saying, "The only reason I'm here is that I don't yet have the moral courage to turn down the money." In interviews, he repeatedly stated that becoming "simply a movie actor" was the thing furthest from his thoughts. "I may do a picture now and then," he said on

one occasion, "but mostly I intend to work on the stage." However, he followed *The Men,* which was more of a *succès d'estime* than a commercial triumph, by recreating Kowalski in the screen treatment of *A Streetcar Named Desire,* and this role, as it had done on Broadway, established him as a star. (Defined practically, a movie star is any performer who can account for a box-office profit regardless of the quality of the enterprise in which he appears; the breed is so scarce that there are fewer than ten actors today who qualify for the title. Brando is one of them; as a box-office draw, male division, he is perhaps outranked only by William Holden.) In the course of the last five years, he has played a Mexican revolutionary (*Viva Zapata!*), Mark Antony (*Julius Caesar*), and a motorcycle-mad juvenile delinquent (*The Wild One*); earned an Academy Award in the role of a dockyard thug (*On the Waterfront*); impersonated Napoleon (*Désirée*); sung and danced his way through the part of an adult delinquent (*Guys and Dolls*); and taken the part of the Okinawan interpreter in *The Teahouse of the August Moon,* which, like *Sayonara,* his tenth picture, was partly shot on location in Japan. But he has never, except for a brief period in summer stock, returned to the stage. "Why should I?" he asked with apathy when I remarked on this. "The movies have a greater potential. They can be a factor for good. For moral development. At least some can—the kind of movies I want to do." He paused, seemed to listen, as though his statement had been tape-recorded and he were now playing it back. Possibly the sound of it dissatisfied him; at any rate, his jaw started working, as if he were biting down on an unpleasant mouthful. He looked off into space suddenly and demanded, "What's so hot about New York? What's so hot about working for Cheryl Crawford and Robert Whitehead?" Miss Crawford and Whitehead are two of New York's most prominent theatrical producers, neither of whom has had occasion to employ Brando. "Anyway, what would I be in?" he continued. "There aren't any parts for me."

Stack them, and the playscripts offered him in any given season by hopeful Broadway managements might very well rise to a height exceeding the actor's own. Tennessee Williams wanted him for the male lead in each of his last five plays, and the most recent of these, *Orpheus Descending,* which was pending production at the time of our talk, had been written expressly as a co-starring vehicle for Brando and the Italian actress Anna Magnani. "I can explain very easily why I didn't do *Orpheus,*" Brando said. "There are beautiful things in it, some of Tennessee's best writing, and the Magnani part is great; she stands for something, you can understand her—and she would wipe me off the stage. The character I was supposed to play, this boy, this Val, he never takes a stand. I didn't really know what he was for or against. Well, you can't act a vacuum. And I told Tennessee. So he kept trying. He rewrote it for me, maybe a couple of times. But—" He shrugged. "Well, I had no intention of walking out on any stage with Magnani. Not in that part. They'd have had to mop me up." Brando mused a moment, and added, "I think—in fact, I'm sure—Tennessee has made a fixed association between me and Kowalski. I mean, we're friends and he knows that as a person I am just the opposite of Kowalski, who was everything I'm against—totally insensitive, crude, cruel. But still Tennessee's image of me is confused with the fact that I played that part. So I don't know if he could write for me in a different color range. The only reason I did *Guys and Dolls* was to work in a lighter color—yellow. Before that, the brightest color I'd played was red. From red down. Brown. Gray. Black." He crumpled an empty cigarette package and bounced it in his hand like a ball. "There aren't any parts for me on the stage.

Nobody writes them. Go on. Tell me a part I could do."

In the absence of vehicles by worthy contemporaries, might he not favor the work of older hands? Several responsible persons who appeared with him in the film had admired his reading of Mark Antony in *Julius Caesar,* and thought him equipped, provided the will was there, to essay many of the Mount Everest roles in stage literature—even, possibly, Oedipus.

Brando received reminders of this praise blankly—or, rather, he seemed to be indulging his not-listening habit. But, sensing silence again, he dissolved it: "Of course, movies *date* so quickly. I saw *Streetcar* the other day and it was already an old-fashioned picture. Still, movies do have the greatest potential. You can say important things to a lot of people. About discrimination and hatred and prejudice. I want to make pictures that explore the themes current in the world today. In terms of entertainment. That's why I've started my own independent production company." He reached out affectionately to finger *A Burst of Vermilion,* which will be the first script filmed by Pennebaker Productions—the independent company he has formed.

And did *A Burst of Vermilion* satisfy him as a basis for the kind of lofty aims he proposed?

He mumbled something. Then he mumbled something else. Asked to speak more clearly, he said, "It's a Western."

He was unable to restrain a smile, which expanded into laughter. He rolled on the floor and roared. "Christ, the only thing is, will I ever be able to look my friends in the face again?" Sobering somewhat, he said, "Seriously, though, the first picture *has* to make money. Otherwise, there won't be another. I'm nearly broke. No, no kidding. I spent a year and two hundred thousand dollars of my own money trying to get some writer to come up with a decent script. Which used my ideas. The last one, it was so terrible I said I can do better myself. I'm going to direct it, too."

Produced by, directed by, written by, and staring. Charlie Chaplin has managed this, and gone it one better by composing his own scores. But professionals of wide experience—Orson Welles, for one—have caved in under a lesser number of chores than Brando planned to assume. However, he had a ready answer to my suggestion that he might be loading the cart with more than the donkey could haul. "Take producing," he said. "What does a producer do except cast? I know as much about casting as anyone does, and that's all producing is. Casting." In the trade, one would be hard put to it to find anyone who concurred in this opinion. A good producer, in addition to doing the casting— that is, assembling the writer, the director, the actors, the technical crew, and the other components of his team—must be a diplomat of the emotions, smoothing and soothing, and above all, must be a skilled mechanic when it comes to dollars-and-cents machinery. "But seriously," said Brando, now excessively sober, "*Burst isn't* just cowboys-and-Indians stuff. It's about this Mexican boy—hatred and discrimination. What happens to a community when those things exist."

Sayonara, too, has moments when it purports to attack race prejudice, telling, as it does, the tale of an American jet pilot who falls in love with a Japanese music-hall dancer, much to the dismay of his Air Force superiors, and also to the dismay of her employers, though the latter's objection is not the racial unsuitability of her beau but simply that she has a beau at all, for she is a member of an all-girl opera company—based on a real-life counterpart, the Takarazuka Company—whose management promotes a legend that offstage its hundreds of girls

lead a conventlike existence, unsullied by male presences of any creed or color. Michener's novel concludes with the lovers forlornly bidding each other *sayonara,* a word meaning farewell. In the film version, however, the word, and consequently the title, has lost significance; here the fadeout reveals the twain of East and West so closely met that they are on their way to the matrimonial bureau. At a press conference that Brando conducted upon his Tokyo arrival, he informed some sixty reporters that he had contracted to do this story because "it strikes very precisely at prejudices that serve to limit our progress toward a peaceful world. Underneath the romance, it attacks prejudices that exist on the part of the Japanese as well as on our part," and also he was doing the film because it would give him the "invaluable opportunity" of working under Joshua Logan, who could teach him "what to do and what not to do."

But time had passed. And now Brando said, with a snort, "Oh, *Sayonara,* I love it! This wondrous hearts-and-flowers nonsense that was supposed to be a serious picture about Japan. So what difference does it make? I'm just doing it for the money anyway. Money to put in the kick for my own company." He pulled at his lip reflectively and snorted again. "Back in California, I sat through twenty-two hours of script conferences. Logan said to me, 'We welcome any suggestions you have, Marlon. Any changes you want to make, you just make them. If there's anything you don't like—why, rewrite it, Marlon, write it your own way.'" Brando's friends boast that he can imitate anybody after fifteen minutes' observation; to judge by the eerie excellence with which he mimicked Logan's vaguely Southern voice, his sad-eyed, beaming, aquiver-with-enthusiasm manner, they are hardly exaggerating. *"Rewrite?* Man, I rewrote the whole damn script. And now out of that they're going to use maybe eight lines." Another snort. "I give up, I'm going to walk through the part, and that's that. Sometimes I think nobody knows the difference anyway. For the first few days on the set, I tried to act. But then I made an experiment. In this scene, I tried to do everything wrong I could think of. Grimaced and rolled my eyes, put in all kinds of gestures and expressions that had no relation to the part I'm supposed to be playing. What did Logan say? He just said, 'It's wonderful! Print it!'"

A phrase that often occurs in Brando's conversation, "I only mean forty per cent of what I say," is probably applicable here. Logan, a stage and film director of widely recognized and munificently rewarded accomplishments (*Mister Roberts, South Pacific, Picnic*), is a man balanced on enthusiasm, as a bird is balanced on air. A creative person's need to believe in the value of what he is creating is axiomatic; Logan's belief in whatever project he is engaged in approaches euphoric faith, protecting him, as it seems designed to do, from the nibbling nuisance of self-doubt. The joy he took in everything connected with *Sayonara,* a film he had been preparing for two years, was so nearly flawless that it did not permit him to conceive that his star's enthusiasm might not equal his own. Far from it. "Marlon," he occasionally announced, "says he's never been as happy with a company as he is with us." And "I've never worked with such an exciting, inventive actor. So pliable. He takes direction beautifully, and yet he always has something to add. He's made up this Southern accent for the part; I never would have thought of it myself, but, well, it's exacly right—it's perfection." Nevertheless, by the night I had dinner in Brando's hotel room Logan had begun to be aware that there was something lacking in his rapport with Brando. He attributed it to the fact that at this juncture, when most of the scenes being filmed concentrated on Japanese background

(street crowds, views, spectacles) rather than actors, he had not yet worked with Brando on material that put either of them to much of a test. "That'll come when we get back to California," he said. "The interior stuff, the dramatic scenes. Brando's going to be great—we'll get along fine."[...]

At that moment, in the Miyako, Brando was presented with something Japanese to enjoy: an emissary of the hotel management, who, bowing and beaming and soaping his hands, came into the room saying "Ah, Missa Marron Brando—" and was silent, tongue-tied by the awkwardness of his errand. He'd come to reclaim the "gift" packages of candy and rice cakes that Brando had already opened and avidly sampled. "Ah, Missa Marron Brando, it is a missake. They were meant for derivery in another room. Aporogies! Aporogies!" Laughing, Brando handed the boxes over. The eyes of the emissary, observing the plundered contents, grew grave, though his smile lingered—indeed, became fixed. Here was a predicament to challenge the rightly renowned Japanese politeness. "Ah," he breathed, a solution limbering his smile, "since you rike them very much, you muss keep one box." He handed the rice cakes back. "And they"—apparently the rightful owner—"can have the other. So, now everyone is preased."

It was just as well that he left the rice cakes, for dinner was taking a long while to simmer in the kitchen. When it arrived, I was replying to some inquiries Brando had made about an acquaintance of mine, a young American disciple of Buddhism who for five years had been leading a contemplative, if not entirely unworldly, life in a settlement inside the gates of Kyoto's Nishi-Honganji Temple. The notion of a person's retiring from the world to lead a spiritual existence—an Oriental one, at that—made Brando's face become still, in a dreaming way. He listened with surprising attention to what I could tell him about the young man's present life, and was puzzled—chagrined, really—that it was not at all, or at all, a matter of withdrawal, of silence and prayer-sore knees. On the contrary, behind Nishi-Honganji's walls my Buddhist friend occupied three snug, sunny rooms brimming with books and phonograph records; along with attending to his prayers and performing the tea ceremony, he was quite capable of mixing a Martini; he had two servants, and a Chevrolet, in which he often conveyed himself to the local cinemas. And, speaking of that, he had read that Marlon Brando was in town, and longed to meet him. Brando was little amused. The puritan streak in him, which has some width, had been touched; his conception of the truly devout could not encompass anyone as *du monde* as the young man I'd described. "It's like the other day on the set," he said. "We were working in a temple, and one of the monks came over and asked me for an autographed picture. Now, *what* would a monk want with my autograph? A picture of me?"

He stared questioningly at his scattered books, so many of which dealt with mystical subjects. At his first Tokyo press conference, he had told the journalists that he was glad to be back in Japan, because it gave him another chance to "investigate the influence" of Buddhism on Japanese thought, the determining cultural factor." The reading matter on display offered proof that he was adhering to this scholarly, if somewhat obscure, program. "What I'd like to do," he presently said, "I'd like to talk to someone who *knows* about these things. Because—" But the explanation was deferred until the maid, who just then skated in balancing vast platters, had set the lacquer table and we had knelt on cushions at either end of it.

"Because," he resumed, wiping his hands on a small steamed towel, the usual preface to any meal served in Japan, "I've seriously considered—I've

very *seriously* thought about—throwing the whole thing up. This business of being a successful actor. What's the point, if it doesn't evolve into anything? All right, you're a success. At last you're *accepted,* you're welcome everywhere. But that's it, that's all there is to it, it doesn't lead anywhere. You're just sitting on a pile of candy gathering thick layers of—of *crust.*" He rubbed his chin with the towel, as though removing stale makeup. "Too much success can ruin you as surely as too much failure." Lowering his eyes, he looked without appetite at the food that the maid, to an accompaniment of constant giggles, was distributing on the plates. "Of course," he said hesitantly, as if he were slowly turning over a coin to study the side that seemed to be shinier, "you can't *always* be a failure. Not and survive. Van Gogh! There's an example of what can happen when a person never receives any recognition. You stop relating; it puts you outside. But I guess success does that, too. You know, it took me a long time before I was aware that that's what I was—a big success. I was so absorbed in myself, my own problems, I never looked around, took account. I used to walk in New York, miles and miles, walk in the streets late at night, and never *see* anything. I was never sure about acting, whether that was what I really wanted to do; I'm still not. Then, when I was in *Streetcar,* and it had been running a couple of months, one night—dimly, dimly—I began to hear this roar. It was like I'd been asleep, and I woke up here sitting on a pile of candy."

Before Brando achieved this sugary perch, he had known the vicissitudes of any unconnected, unfinanced, only partly educated (he has never received a high-school diploma, having been expelled before graduation from Shattuck Military Academy, in Faribault, Minnesota, an institution he refers to as "the asylum") young man who arrives in New York from more rural parts—in his case, Libertyville,

Illinois. Living alone in furnished rooms, or sharing underfurnished apartments, he had spent his first city years fluctuating between acting classes and a fly-by-night enrollment in Social Security; Best's once had him on its payroll as an elevator boy. A friend of his, who saw a lot of him in those pre-candy days, corroborates to some extent the rather somnambulistic portrait Brando paints of himself. "He was a brooder, all right," the friend has said. "He seemed to have a built-in hideaway room and was always rushing off to it to worry over himself, and gloat, too, like a miser with his gold. But it wasn't all Gloomsville. When he wanted to, he could rocket right out of himself. He had a wild, kid kind of fun thing. Once, he was living in an old brown-stone on Fifty-second Street, near where some of the jazz joints are. He used to go up on the roof and fill paper bags with water and throw them down at the stiffs coming out of the clubs. He had a sign on the wall of his room that said, 'You Ain't Livin' If You Don't Know It.' Yeah, there was always some-thing jumping in that apartment—Marlon playing the bongos, records going, people around, kids from the Actors' Studio, and a lot of down-and-outers he'd picked up. And he could be sweet. He was the least opportunistic person I've ever known. He never gave a damn about anybody who could help him; you might say he went out of his way to avoid them. Sure, part of that—the kind of people he didn't like and the kind he did, both—stemmed from his insecurities, his inferiority feelings. Very few of his friends were his equals—anybody he'd have to *compete* with, if you know what I mean. Mostly they were strays, idolizers, characters who were dependent on him one way or another. The same with the girls he took out. Plain sort of somebody's-secretary-type girls—nice enough but nothing that's going to start a stampede of competitors." (The last-mentioned preference of Brando's was true of him as an adolescent, too, or so his grandmother has said. As she put it, "Marlon always picked on the cross-eyed girls.")

The maid poured *sake* into thimble-size cups, and withdrew. Connoisseurs of this palely pungent rice wine pretend they can discern variations in taste and quality in over fifty brands. But to the novice all *sake* seems to have been brewed in the same vat—a toddy, pleasant at first, cloying afterward, and not likely to echo in your head unless it is devoured by the quart, a habit many of Japan's *bons vivants* have adopted. Brando ignored the *sake* and went straight for his filet. The steak was excellent; Japanese take a just pride in the quality of their beef. The spaghetti, a dish that is very popular in Japan, was not; nor was the rest—the conglomeration of peas, potatoes, beans. Granted that the menu was a queer one, it is on the whole a mistake to order Western-style food in Japan, yet there arise those moments when one retches at the thought of more raw fish, sukiyaki, and rice with seaweed, when, however temptingly they may be prepared and however prettily pres-ented, the unaccustomed stomach revolts at the prospect of eel broth and fried bees and pickled snake and octopus arms.

As we ate, Brando returned to the possibility of renouncing his movie-star status for the satisfactions of a life that "led somewhere." He decided to compromise. "Well, when I get back to Hollywood, what I *will* do, I'll fire my secretary and move into a smaller house," he said. He sighed with relief, as though he'd already cast off old encumbrances and entered upon the simplicities of his new situation. Embroidering on its charms, he said, "I won't have a cook or maid. Just a cleaning woman who comes in twice a week. But"—he frowned, squinted, as if something were blurring the bliss he envisioned—"wherever the house is, it has to have a *fence*. On account of the people with pencils. You don't know what it's like. The people with pencils. I need a fence to keep them out. I suppose there's nothing I can do about the telephone."

"Telephone?"

"It's tapped. Mine is."

"Tapped? Really? By whom?"

He chewed his steak, mumbled. He seemed reluctant to say, yet certain it was so. "When I talk to my friends, we speak French. Or else a kind of bop lingo we made up."

Suddenly, sounds came through the ceiling from the room above us—footfalls, muffled voices like the noise of water flowing through a pipe. "Sh-h-h!" whispered Brando, listening intently, his gaze alerted upward. "Keep your voice down. *They* can hear everything." They, it appeared, were his fellow actor Red Buttons and Buttons' wife, who occupied the suite overhead. "This place is made of paper," he continued, in tiptoe tones, and with the absorbed countenance of a child lost in a very earnest game—an expression that half explained his secretiveness, the looking-over-his-shoulder, coded-bop-for-telephones facet of his personality that occasionally causes conversation with him to assume a conspiratorial quality, as though one were discussing subversive topics in perilous political territory. Brando said nothing; I said nothing. Nor did Mr. and Mrs. Button—not anything distinguishable. During the siege of silence, my host located a letter buried among the dinner plates, and read it while he ate, like a gentleman perusing his breakfast newspaper. Presently, remembering me, he remarked, "From a friend of mine. He's making a documentary, the life of James Dean. He wants me to do the narration. I think I might." He tossed the letter aside and pulled his apple pie, topped with a melting scoop of vanilla ice cream, toward him. "Maybe not, though. I get excited about something, but it never lasts more than seven minutes. Seven minutes exactly. That's my limit. I never know why I get up in the morning." Finishing his pie, he gazed speculatively at my portion; I passed it to him. "But I'm really considering this Dean thing. It could be important."

James Dean, the young motion-picture actor killed in a car accident in 1955, was promoted throughout his phosphorescent career as the All-American "mixed-up kid," the symbol of misunderstood hot-rodding youth with a switch-blade approach to life's little problems. When he died, an expensive film in which he had starred, *Giant,* had yet to be released, and the picture's press agents, seeking to offset any ill effects that Dean's demise might have on the commercial prospects of their product, succeeded by "glamorizing" the tragedy, and, in ironic consequence, created a Dean legend of rather necrophilic appeal. Though Brando was seven years older than Dean, and professionally more secure, the two actors came to be associated in the collective movie-fan mind. Many critics reviewing Dean's first film, *East of Eden,* remarked on the well-nigh plagiaristic resemblance between his acting mannerisms and Brando's. Offscreen, too, Dean appeared to be practicing the sincerest form of flattery; like Brando, he tore around on motorcycles, played bongo drums, dressed the role of rowdy, spouted an intellectual rigmarole, cultivated a cranky, colorful newspaper personality that mingled, to a skillfully potent degree, plain bad boy and sensitive sphinx.

"No, Dean was never a friend of mine," said Brando, in response to a question that he seemed surprised to have been asked. "That's not why I may do the narration job. I hardly knew him. But he had an *idée fixe* about me. Whatever I did he did. He was always trying to get close to me. He used to call up." Brando lifted an imaginary telephone, put it to his ear with a cunning, eavesdropper's smile. "I'd listen to him talking to the answering service, asking where the customers wore shoes. "We're just finishing. How about it? You through?"

Brando looked at me thoughtfully, and I, in turn, at my coat. But he said, "We're still yakking. Call me back in an hour."

O.K. Well . . . O.K. Listen. Miiko's here. She wants to know did you get the flowers she sent you?"

Brando's eyes lazily rolled toward the glassed-in sun porch, where a bowl of asters was centered on a round bamboo table. "Uh-huh. Tell her thanks very much."

"Tell her yourself. She's right here."

"No! Hey, wait a minute! Christ, *that's* not how you do it." But the protest came too late. Murray had already put down the phone, and Brando, reiterating *"That's* not how you do it," blushed and squirmed like an embarrassed boy.

The next voice to emanate from the receiver belonged to his *Sayonara* leading lady, Miss Miiko Taka. She asked about his health.

"Better, thanks. I ate the bad end of an oyster, that's all. Miiko? . . . Miiko, that was very *sweet* of you to send me the flowers. They're beautiful. I'm looking at them right now. Asters," he continued, as though shyly venturing a line of verse, "are my favorite flowers. . . ."

I retired to the sun porch, leaving Brando and Miss Taka to conduct their conversation in stricter seclusion. Below the windows, the hotel garden, with its ultrasimple and *soigné* arrangements of rock and tree, floated in the mists that crawl off Kyoto's waterways—for it *is* a watery city, crisscrossed with shallow rivers and cascading canals, dotted with pools as still as coiled snakes and mirthful little waterfalls that sound like Japanese girls giggling. Once the imperial capital and now the country's cultural museum, such an aesthetic treasure house that American bombers let it go unmolested during

the war, Kyoto is surrounded by water, too; beyond the city's containing hills, thin roads run like causeways across the reflecting silver of flooded rice fields. That evening, despite the gliding mists, the blue encircling hills were discernible against the night, for the upper air had purity; a sky was there, stars were in it, and a scrap of moon. Some portions of the town could be seen. Nearest was a neighborhood of curving roofs, the dark façades of aristocratic houses fashioned from silky wood yet austere, northern, as secret-looking as any stone Siena palace. How brilliant they made the street lamps appear, and the doorway lanterns casting keen kimono colors—pink and orange, lemon and red. Farther away was a modern flatness—wide avenues and neon, a skyscraper of raw concrete that seemed less enduring, more perishable, than the papery dwellings stooping around it.

Brando completed his call. Approaching the sun porch, he looked at me looking at the view. He said, "Have you been to Nara? Pretty interesting."

I had, and yes, it was. "Ancient, old-time Nara," as a local cicerone unfailingly referred to it, is an hour's drive from Kyoto—a postcard town set in a show-place park. Here is the apotheosis of the Japanese genius for hypnotizing nature into unnatural behavior. The great shrine-infested park is a green salon where sheep graze, and herds of tame deer wander under trim pine trees and, like Venetian pigeons, gladly pose with honeymooning couples; where children yank the beards of unretaliating goats; where old men wearing black capes with mink collars squat on the shores of lotus-quilted lakes and, by clapping their hands, summon swarms of fish, speckled and scarlet carp, fat, thick as trout, who allow their snouts to be tickled, then gobble the crumbs that the old men sprinkle. That this serpentless Eden should strongly appeal to Brando was a bit surprising. With his liberal taste for the off-trail and not-overly-trammeled, one might have thought he would be unresponsive to so ruly, subjugated a landscape. Then, as though apropos of Nara, he said, "Well, I'd like to be married. I want to have children." It was not, perhaps, the non sequitur it seemed; the gentle safety of Nara just could, by the association of ideas, suggest marriage, a family.

"You've got to have love," he said. "There's no other reason for living. Men are no different from mice. They're born to perform the same function. Procreate." ("Marlon," to quote his friend Elia Kazan, "is one of the gentlest people I've ever known. Possibly the gentlest." Kazan's remark had meaning when one observed Brando in the company of children. As far as he was concerned, Japan's youngest generation—lovely, lively, cherry-cheeked kids with bowlegs and bristling bangs—was always welcome to lark around the *Sayonara* sets. He was good with the children, at ease, playful, appreciative; he seemed, indeed, for me, leaving messages. But I never spoke up. I never called him back. No, when I—"

The scene was interrupted by the ringing of a real telephone. "Yeah?" he said, picking it up. "Speaking. From where? . . . Manila? . . . Well, I don't know anybody in Manila. Tell them I'm not here. No, when I finally met Dean," he said, hanging up, "it was at a party. Where he was throwing himself around, acting the madman. So I spoke to him. I took him aside and asked him didn't he know he was sick? That he needed help?" The memory evoked an intensified version of Brando's familiar look of enlightened compassion. "He listened to me. He knew he was sick. I gave him the name of an analyst, and he went. And at least his *work* improved. Toward the end, I think he was beginning to find his own way as an actor. But this glorifying of Dean is all wrong. That's why I believe the documentary could be important. To show he wasn't

a hero; show what he really was—just a lost boy trying to find himself. That ought to be done, and I'd like to do it—maybe as a kind of expiation for some of my own sins. Like making *The Wild One.*" He was referring to the strange film in which he was presented as the Führer of a tribe of Fascistlike delinquents. "But. Who knows? Seven minutes is my limit." From Dean the conversation turned to other actors, and I asked which ones, specifically, Brando respected. He pondered; though his lips shaped several names, he seemed to have second thoughts about pronouncing them. I suggested a few candidates—Laurence Olivier, John Gielgud, Montgomery Clift, Gérard Philipe, Jean-Louis Barrault. "Yes," he said, at last coming alive, "Philipe is a good actor. So is Barrault. Christ, what a wonderful picture that was—*Les Enfants du Paradis!* Maybe the best movie ever made. You know, that's the only time I ever fell in love with an actress, somebody on the screen. I was mad about Arletty." The Parisian star Arletty is well remembered by international audiences for the witty, womanly allure she brought to the heroine's part in Barrault's celebrated film. "I mean, I was really in *love* with her. My first trip to Paris, the thing I did right away, I asked to meet Arletty. I went to see her as though I were going to a shrine. My ideal woman. Wow!" He slapped the table. "Was that a mistake, was that a disillusionment! She was a tough article."

The maid came to clear the table; *en passant,* she gave Brando's shoulder a sisterly pat, rewarding him, I took it, for the cleaned-off sparkle of his plates. He again collapsed on the floor, stuffing a pillow under his head. "I'll tell you," he said, "Spencer Tracy is the kind of actor I like to watch. The way he holds back, *holds* back—then darts in to make his point, darts back. Tracy, Muni, Cary Grant. They know what they're doing. You can learn something from them."

Brando began to weave his fingers in the air, as though hoping that gestures would describe what he could not precisely articulate. "Acting is such a tenuous thing," he said. "A fragile, shy thing that a sensitive director can help lure out of you. Now, in movie-acting the important, the *sensitive* moment comes around the third take of a scene; by then you just need a whisper from the director to crystallize it for you. Gadge"—he was using Elia Kazan's nickname—"can usually do it. He's wonderful with actors."

Another actor, I suppose, would have understood at once what Brando was saying, but I found him difficult to follow. "It's what happens inside you on the third take," he said, with a careful emphasis that did not lessen my incomprehension. One of the most memorable film scenes Brando has played occurs in the Kazan-directed *On the Waterfront;* it is the car-ride scene in which Rod Steiger, as the racketeering brother, confesses he is leading Brando into a death trap. I asked if he could use the episode as an example, and tell me how his theory of the "sensitive moment" applied to it.

"Yes. Well, no. Well, let's see." He puckered his eyes, made a humming noise. "That was a seven-take scene, and I didn't like the way it was written. Lot of dissension going on there. I was fed up with the whole picture. All the location stuff was in New Jersey, and it was the dead of winter—the cold, Christ! And I was having problems at the time. Woman trouble. That scene. Let me see. There were seven takes because Rod Steiger couldn't stop crying. He's one of those actors loves to cry. We kept doing it over and over. But I can't remember just when, just how it crystallized itself for me. The first time I saw *Waterfront,* in a projection room with Gadge, I thought it was so terrible I walked out without even speaking to him."

A month earlier, a friend of Brando's had told me,

"Marlon always turns against whatever he's working on. Some element of it. Either the script or the director or somebody in the cast. Not always because of anything very rational—just because it seems to comfort him to be dissatisfied, let off steam about something. It's part of his pattern. Take *Sayonara.* A dollar gets you ten he'll develop a hoss on it somewhere along the line. A hoss on Logan, maybe. Maybe against Japan—the whole damn country. He loves Japan *now.* But with Marlon you never know from one minute to the next."

I was wondering whether I might mention this supposed "pattern" to Brando, ask if he considered it a valid observation about himself. But it was as though he had anticipated the question. "I ought to keep my mouth shut," he said. "Around here, around *Sayonara,* I've let a few people know the way I feel. But I don't always feel the same way two days running."

It was ten-thirty, and Murray called on the dot.

"I went out to dinner with the girls," he told Brando, his telephone voice so audible that I could hear it, too; it spoke above a blend of dance-band rumble and barroom roar. Obviously he was patronizing not one of the more traditional, cat-quiet Kyoto restaurants but, rather, a place their emotional contemporary, a co-conspirator. Moreover, the condoling expression, the slight look of dispensing charitable compassion, peculiar to his contemplation of some adults was absent from his eyes when he looked at a child.)

Touching Miss Taka's floral offering, he went on, "What other reason is there for living? Except love? That has been my main trouble. My inability to love anyone." He turned back into the lighted room, stood there as though hunting something—a cigarette? He picked up a pack. Empty. He slapped at the pockets of trousers and jackets lying here and there. Brando's wardrobe no longer smacks of the street gang; as a dresser, he has graduated, or gone back, into an earlier style of outlaw chic, that of the prohibition sharpie—black snap-brim hats, striped suits, and somber-hued George Raft shirts with pastel ties. Cigarettes were found; inhaling, he slumped on the pallet bed. Beads of sweat ringed his mouth. The electric heater hummed. The room was tropical; one could have grown orchids. Overhead, Mr. and Mrs. Buttons were again bumping about, but Brando appeared to have lost interest in them. He was smoking, thinking. Then, picking up the stitch of his thought, he said, "I can't. Love anyone. I can't trust anyone enough to give myself to them. But I'm ready. I want it. And I may, I'm almost on the point, I've really got to . . ." His eyes narrowed, but his tone, far from being intense, was indifferent, dully objective, as though he were discussing some character in a play—a part he was weary of portraying yet was trapped in by contract. "Because—well, what else is there? That's all it's all about. To love somebody."

(At this time, Brando was, of course, a bachelor, who had, upon occasion, indulged in engagements of a quasi-official character—once to an aspiring authoress and actress, by name Miss Blossom Plumb, and again, with more public attention, to Mlle. Josanne Mariani-Bérenger, a French fisherman's daughter. But in neither instance were banns ever posted. One day last month, however, in a sudden and somewhat secret ceremony at Eagle Rock, California, Brando was married to a dark sari-swathed young minor actress who called herself Anna Kashfi. According to conflicting press reports, either she was a Darjeeling-born Buddhist of the purest Indian parentage or she was the Calcutta-born daughter of an English couple named O'Callaghan, now living in Wales. Brando has not yet done anything to clear up the mystery.)

"Anyway, I have *friends*. No. No, I don't," he

said, verbally shadowboxing. "Oh, sure I do," he decided, smoothing the sweat on his upper lip. "I have a great many friends. Some I don't hold out on. I let them know what's happening. You have to trust somebody. Well, not all the way. There's nobody I rely on to tell *me* what to do."

I asked if that included professional advisers. For instance, it was my understanding that Brando very much depended on the guidance of Jay Kanter, a young man on the staff of the Music Corporation of America, which is the agency that represents him. "Oh, Jay," Brando said now. "Jay does what I tell *him* to. I'm alone like that."

The telephone sounded. An hour seemed to have passed, for it was Murray again. "Yeah, still yakking," Brando told him. "Look, let *me* call you. . . . Oh, in an hour or so. You be back in your room?. . . O.K."

He hung up, and said, "Nice guy. He wants to be a director—eventually. I was saying something, though. We were talking about friends. Do you know how I make a friend?" He leaned a little toward me, as though he had an amusing secret to impart. "I go about it very gently. I circle around and around. I circle. Then, gradually, I come nearer. Then I reach out and touch them—ah, so gently . . ." His fingers stretched forward like insect feelers and grazed my arm. "Then," he said, one eye half shut, the other, à la Rasputin, mesmerically wide and shining, "I draw back. Wait awhile. Make them wonder. At just the right moment, I move in again. Touch them. Circle." Now his hand, broad and blunt-fingered, traveled in a rotating pattern, as though it held a rope with which he was binding an invisible presence. "They don't know what's happening. Before they realize it, they're all entangled, involved. I have them. And suddenly, sometimes, I'm all *they* have. A lot of them, you see, are people who don't fit anywhere; they're not accepted, they've been hurt, crippled one way or another. But I want to help them, and they can focus on me; I'm the duke. Sort of the duke of my domain."

(A past tenant on the ducal preserve, describing its seigneur and his subjects, has said, "It's as though Marlon lived in a house where the doors are never locked. When he lived in New York, the door always *was* open. Anybody could come in, whether Marlon was there or not, and everybody did. You'd arrive and there would be ten, fifteen characters wandering around. It was strange, because nobody seemed to really know anybody else. They were just there, like people in a bus station. Some type asleep in a chair. People reading the tabs. A girl dancing by herself. Or painting her toenails. A comedian trying out his night-club act. Off in a corner, there'd be a chess game going. And drums—bang, boom, bang, boom! But there was never any drinking—nothing like that. Once in a while, somebody would say. 'Let's go down to the corner for an ice-cream soda.' Now, in all this Marlon was the common de-nominator, the only connecting link. He'd move around the room drawing individuals aside and talking to them alone. If you've noticed, Marlon can't, *won't*, talk to two people simultaneously. He'll never take part in a *group* conversation. It always has to be a cozy tête-à-tête—one person at a time. Which is necessary, I suppose, if you use the same kind of charm on everyone. But even when you know that's what he's doing, it doesn't matter. Because when *your* turn comes, he makes you feel you're the only person in the room. In the world. Makes you feel that you're under his protection and that your troubles and moods concern him deeply. You have to believe it; more than anyone I've known, he radiates *sincerity*. Aferward, you may ask yourself, 'Is it an act?' If so, what's the point? What have you got to give him? Nothing except—and this *is* the point—affection. Affection that lends him

authority over you. I sometimes think Marlon is like an orphan who later on in life tries to compensate by becoming the kindly head of a huge orphanage. But even outside this institution he wants everybody to love him." Although there exist a score of witnesses who might well contradict the last opinion, Brando himself is credited with having once informed an interviewer, "I can walk into a room where there are a hundred people—if there is *one* person in that room who doesn't like me, I know it and have to get out." As a footnote, it should be added that within the clique over which Brando presides he is esteemed as an intellectual father, as well as an emotional big brother. The person who probably knows him best, the comedian Wally Cox, declares him to be "a creative philosopher, a very deep thinker," and adds. "He's a real liberating force for his friends.")

Brando yawned; it had got to be a quarter past one. In less than five hours he would have to be showered, shaved, breakfasted, on the set, and ready for a makeup man to paint his pale face the mulatto tint that Technicolor requires.

"Let's have another cigarette," he said as I made a move to put on my coat.

"Don't you think you should go to sleep?"

"That just means getting up. Most mornings, I don't know why I do. I can't face it." He looked at the telephone, as though remembering his promise to call Murray. "Anyway, I may work later on. You want something to drink?"

Outside, the stars had darkened and it had started to drizzle, so the prospect of a nightcap was pleasing, especially if I should have to return on foot to my own hotel, which was a mile distant from the Miyako. I poured some vodka; Brando declined to join me. However, he subsequently reached for my glass, sipped from it, set it down between us, and suddenly said, in an offhand way that nonetheless conveyed feeling, "My mother. She broke apart like a piece of porcelain."

I had often heard friends of Brando's say, "Marlon worshiped his mother." But prior to 1947, and the première of *A Streetcar Named Desire*, few, perhaps none, of the young actor's circle had met either of his parents; they knew nothing of his background except what he chose to tell them. "Marlon always gave a very colorful picture of home life back in Illinois," one of his acquaintances told me. "When we heard that his family were coming to New York for the opening of *Streetcar*, everybody was very curious. We didn't know what to expect. On opening night, Irene Selznick gave a big party at '21.' Marlon came with his mother and father. Well, you can't imagine two more attractive people. Tall, handsome, charming as they could be. What impressed me—I think it amazed everyone—was Marlon's attitude toward them. In their presence, he wasn't the lad we knew. He was a model son. Reticent, respectful, very polite, considerate in every way."

Born in Omaha, Nebarska, where his father was a salesman of limestone products, Brando, the family's third child and only son, was soon taken to live in Libertyville, Illinois. There the Brandos settled down in a rambling house in a countrified neighborhood; at least, there was enough country around the house to allow the Brandos to keep geese and hens and rabbits, a horse, a Great Dane, twenty-eight cats, and a cow. Milking the cow was the daily chore that belonged to Bud, as Marlon was then nicknamed. Bud seems to have been an extroverted and competitive boy. Everyone who came within range of him was at once forced into some variety of contest: Who can eat fastest? Hold his breath longest? Tell the tallest tale? Bud was rebellious, too; rain or shine, he ran away from home every Sunday. But he and his two sisters, Frances and Jocelyn, were

devotedly close to their mother. Many years later, Stella Adler, Brando's former drama coach, described Mrs. Brando, who died in 1954, as "a very beautiful, a heavenly, lost, girlish creature." Always, wherever she lived, Mrs. Brando had played leads in the productions of local dramatic societies, and always she had longed for a more brightly footlighted world than her surroundings provided. These yearings inspired her children. Frances took to painting; Jocelyn, who is at present a professional actress, interested herself in the theatre. Bud, too, had inherited his mother's theatrical inclinations, but at seventeen he announced a wish to study for the ministry. (Then, as now, Brando searched for a belief. As one Brando disciple once summed it up, "He needs to find something in life, something in himself, that is permanently true, and he needs to lay down his life for it. For such an intense personality, nothing less than that will do.") Talked out of his clerical ambitions, expelled from school, rejected for military service in 1942 because of a trick knee, Brando packed up and came to New York. Whereupon Bud, the plump, towheaded, unhappy adolescent, exits, and the man-sized and very gifted Marlon emerges.

Brando has not forgotten Bud. When he speaks of the boy he was, the boy seems to inhabit him, as if time had done little to separate the man from the hurt, desiring child. "My father was indifferent to me," he said. "Nothing I could do interested him, or pleased him. I've accepted that now. We're friends now. We get along." Over the past ten years, the elder Brando has supervised his son's financial affairs; in addition to Pennebaker Productions, of which Mr. Brando, Sr., is an employee, they have been associated in a number of ventures, including a Nebraska grain-and-cattle ranch, in which a large percentage of the younger Brando's earnings was invested. "But my mother was everything to me.

A whole world. I tried so hard. I used to come home from school ..." He hesitated, as though waiting for me to picture him: Bud, books under his arm, scuffling his way along an afternoon street. "There wouldn't be anybody home. Nothing in the icebox." More lantern slides: empty room, a kitchen. "Then the telephone would ring. Somebody calling from some bar. And they'd say. 'We've got a lady down here. You better come get her.'" Suddenly, Brando was silent. In the silence the picture faded, or, rather, became fixed: Bud at the telephone. At last, the image moved again, leaped forward in time. Bud is eighteen, and: "I thought if she loved me enough, trusted me enough, I thought, then we can be together, in New York; we'll live together and I'll take care of her. Once, later on, that really happened. She left my father and came to live with me. In New York, when I was in a play. I tried so hard. But my love wasn't enough. She couldn't care enough. She went back. And one day"—the flatness of his voice grew flatter, yet the emotional pitch ascended until one could discern, like a sound within a sound, a wounded bewilderment—"I didn't care any more. She was there. In a room. Holding on to me. And I let her fall. Because I couldn't take it any more—watch her breaking apart, in front of me, like a piece of porcelain. I stepped right over her. I walked right out. I was indifferent. Since then. I've been indifferent."

The telephone was signaling. Its racket seemed to rouse him from a daze; he stared about, as though he'd wakened in an unknown room, then smiled wryly, then whispered, "Damn, damn, damn," as his hand lurched toward the telephone. "Sorry," he told Murray. "I was just going to call you. ... No, he's leaving now. But look, man, let's call it off tonight. It's after one. It's nearly two o'clock. ... Yeah. ... Sure thing. Tomorrow."   Meanwhile, I'd put on my overcoat, and was waiting to say good night. He walked me to the door, where I put on my shoes.

"Well, *sayonara*," he mockingly bade me. "Tell them at the desk to get you a taxi." Then, as I walked down the corridor, he called, "And listen! Don't pay too much attention to what I say. I don't always feel the same way."

In a sense, this was not my last sight of him that evening. Downstairs, the Miyako's lobby was deserted. There was no one at the desk, nor, outside, were there any taxis in view. Even at high noon, the fancy crochet of Kyoto's streets had played me tricks; still, I set off through the marrow-chilling drizzle in what I hoped was a homeward direction. I'd never before been abroad so late in the city. It was quite a contrast to daytime, when the central parts of the town, caroused by crowds of fiesta massiveness, jangle like the inside of a *pachinko* parlor, or to early evening—Kyoto's most exotic hours, for then, like night flowers, lanterns wreathe the side streets, and resplendent geishas, with their white ceramic faces and their ballooning lacquered wigs strewn with silver bells, their hobbled wiggle-walk, hurry among the shadows toward meticulously tasteful revelries. But at two in the morning these exquisite grotesques are gone, the cabarets are shuttered; only cats remained to keep me company, and drunks and red- light ladies, the inevitable old beggar-bundles in doorways, and, briefly, a ragged street musician who followed me playing on a flute a medieval music. I had trudged far more than a mile when, at last, one of a hundred alleys led to familiar ground—the main-street district of department stores and cinemas. It was then that I saw Brando. Sixty feet tall, with a head as huge as the greatest Buddha's, there he was, in comic-paper colors, on a sign above a theatre that advertised *The Teahouse* of *the August Moon*. Rather Buddha-like, too, was his pose, for he was depicted in a squatting position, a serene smile on a face that glistened in the rain and the light of a street lamp. A deity, yes; but, more than that, really, just a young man sitting on a pile of candy.

The captions to the plates, and the biography providing a table of dates in Marlon Brando's life, are condensed from two majors sources in which Marlon Brando speaks in his own voice: the 1991 volume edited by Lawrence Grobel, *Conversations with Brando* (New York: Hyperion) and from the actor's autobiography, *Brando: Songs My Mother Taught Me* (New York: Random House, 1994).

Additional sources included Tennessee William's *Memoirs* and the book *Marlon Brando—Der versilberte Rebell* by the late Jörg Fauser (Monika Nüchtern, Munich 1978). Jorg Fauser's book, with its very detailed list of sources, uses the fundamental Brando biographies by Bob Thomas, Gary Carey, Carlo Fiore, and Joe Marella / Edward Z. Epstein.

Finally, many valuable insights were gained from Harold Brodkey's review of Marlon Brando's autobiography in the *New Yorker* of 24 October 1994.

Truman Capote's great essay about Marlon Brando, written in 1956 and published in the *New Yorker* in 1957, is reprinted above, slightly shortened, as the introduction; only supplementary remarks are therefore made to it elsewhere.

In general, it should be noted that some of the dates relating to Brando's family history cannot be precisely clarified, since even in his autobiography he gives information that is sometimes contradictory. Marlon Brando's divided feelings about his family are a special phenomenon. For example, he hardly devotes a single word in the autobiography to his children or his wives, while he describes his own childhood with his parents in detail. The biography compiled for the present volume is therefore necessarily incomplete in relation to Brando's marriages, divorces, children, and adopted children.

Daniel Dreier

Plates

"Acting, not prostitution,
is the oldest profession in the world."

Marlon Brando

Portrait of the sensitive young actor in New York, 1946.
Marlon Brando is good-looking, twenty-two years old, and already being tipped as a future star
by insiders on Broadway. He is appearing opposite important actors such as
Katharine Cornell, Tallulah Bankhead, and Paul Muni.

In 1947, during rehearsals for Tennessee William's new play, A Streetcar Named Desire,
*Brando received media attention for the first time. Star photographer Cecil Beaton portrayed him studying
the script (left); Lisa Larsen's double portrait of Marlon Brando and his sister Jocelyn was taken for the report
on the play's première in* Life *magazine. Both photographers give Brando the aura
of an aristocratic young man.*

In his Memoirs, Tennessee Williams recalls the memorable evening in August 1947 when Marlon Brando appeared for his audition:

> Just about this time I got a wire from Kazan, informing me that he was dispatching a young actor to the Cape who he thought was gifted; and he wanted him to read the part of Stanley for me. We waited two or three days, but the young actor, named Marlon Brando, didn't show. I had stopped expecting him when he arrived one evening with a young girl, the kind you would call a chick nowadays.
>
> He asked why the lights weren't on and we told him the electricity had failed. He immediately fixed that for us—I think he merely inserted a penny in the light fuse.
>
> Then he discovered our predicament with the plumbing and he fixed that, too.
>
> He was just about the best-looking young man I've ever seen, with one or two exceptions; but I have never played around with actors, it's a point of morality with me and anyhow Brando was not the type to get a part that way.
>
> When he had gotten the Rancho into shape by repairing the lights and plumbing, he sat down in a corner and started to read the part of Stanley. I was cuing him. After less than ten minutes, Margo Jones jumped up and let out a "Texas Tornado" shout.
>
> "Get Kazan on the phone right away! This is the greatest reading I've ever heard—in or outside of Texas!
>
Brando maybe smiled a little but didn't show any particular elation, such as the elation we all felt.

∽

In a letter to his agent a few days later, Williams described what it was about Brando's reading that had made him so enthusiastic:

> I can't tell you what a relief it is that we have found such a God-sent Stanley in the person of Brando. . . . It humanizes the character of Stanley in that it becomes the brutality or callousness of youth rather than a vicious older man. . . . A new value came out of Brando's reading which was by far the best reading I have ever heard. He seemed to have already created a dimensional character, of the sort that the war has produced among young veterans.

Marlon Brando in T shirt, jeans, and sneakers as Stanley Kowalski in A Streetcar Named Desire.
Stage shot by John Engstead, 1947. He was so convincing in the role of the boorish Kowalski with his unmistakable animal instincts that many of the critics thought he was playing himself. Brando later corrected this misjudgement, which demonstrated the outstanding quality of his acting achievement: "I was the exact opposite of Stanley Kowalski. . . . He was a compendium of my imagination, based on the lines of the play. I created him from Tennessee's words." Stanley Kowalski was Brando's breakthrough to Broadway stardom.

The touching reconciliation scene between Kowalski and Stella from Act I, Scene 3.
Photo by Eliot Elisofon, 1947.

Stage shot with Brando (Kowalski), Kim Hunter (Stella),
and Jessica Tandy (Blanche), 1947. A Streetcar Named Desire *ran for more than two years,*
with a total of 855 performances.

The quality of the newly discovered actor left the audience speechless and exasperated the theatre specialists. Irene Mayer Selznick, who produced the hit play, recalls: "Brando's way of being fully involved on stage had a Zen quality mixed with an obvious narcissism and touches of lunacy and cruelty. Everything he ever did had an element of mockery."

∾

Truman Capote saw him as the "Valentino of the bop generation."

∾

Novelist Harold Brodkey's explanation for the new quality in Brando's acting was the influence of Broadway stars Katharine Cornell and Tallulah Bankhead, whom Brando appeared with early on: "He absorbed their quality, masculinized it slightly, dirtied it and went a bit out of control with it. Brando took over the vanity and posing and sheer willfulness of a good-looking woman and developed a deconstructed version of a diva's romantic sexuality."

Marlon Brando portrait, 1950. Harold Brodkey described the contradictory expression in Brando's eyes: "Clever and androgynous, hauntingly threatening eyes, somehow also soft and weak, satyr/American-stormtrooper eyes."

With the expressed intention of returning to the theatre later on, Brando signed his first movie contract in Hollywood in 1950. Directed by Fred Zinnemann, he played a crippled war veteran in The Men. *He spent several weeks living in a specialist clinic for paraplegic patients in wheelchairs to prepare himself for the part. The picture shows Brando during shooting, with his co-star Teresa Wright (left) and director Fred Zinnemann (right), 1950.*

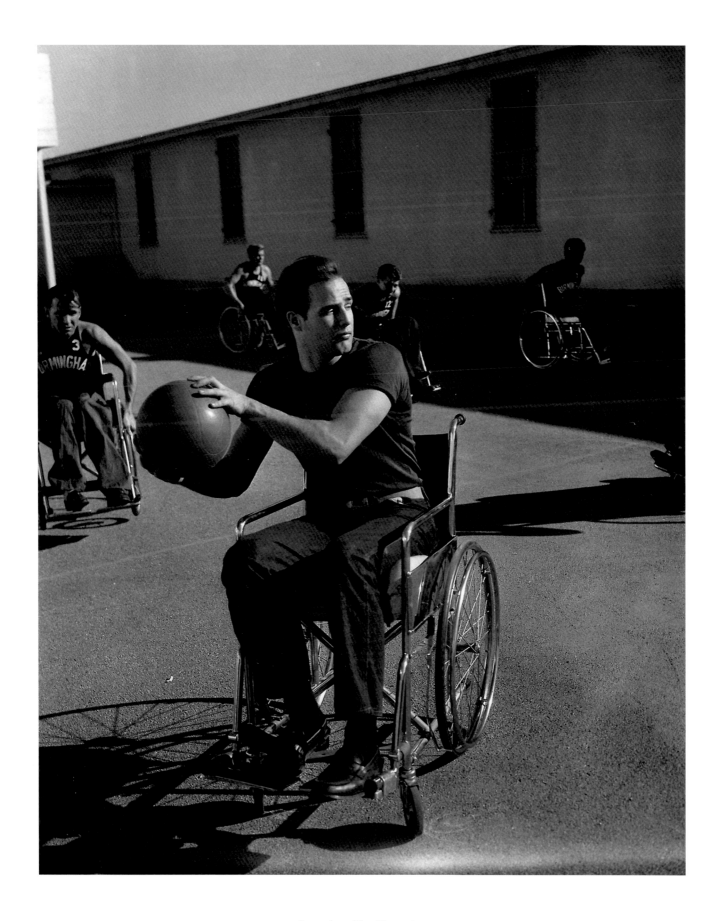

Scene from The Men, *1950.*

Marlon Brando as Ken with his wife in the movie, Teresa Wright, as Ellen.
Scene from The Men, *1950.*

This portrait was taken at the time of Brando's movie debut in The Men.
The publishers of Brando's autobiography liked it so much they used it for the book's
cover photo in 1994.

The film version of A Streetcar Named Desire *brought Brando world stardom in 1951. His proletarian mannerisms as Stanley, and his outfit with the dirty T shirt and jeans, were imitated by the young all over the world. For the director, Elia Kazan,* A Streetcar Named Desire *was the first unsentimental picture ever shot in America. The casting and set were taken from the Broadway production, the only new addition being Vivien Leigh as an already established movie star. The scene shown here shows her in the role of Blanche, with Brando as Stanley.*

Dramatic scene from A Streetcar Named Desire, *1951.*
From left to right: Kim Hunter (Stella), Marlon Brando (Stanley), and Vivien Leigh (Blanche).

Still from A Streetcar Named Desire, *1951.*

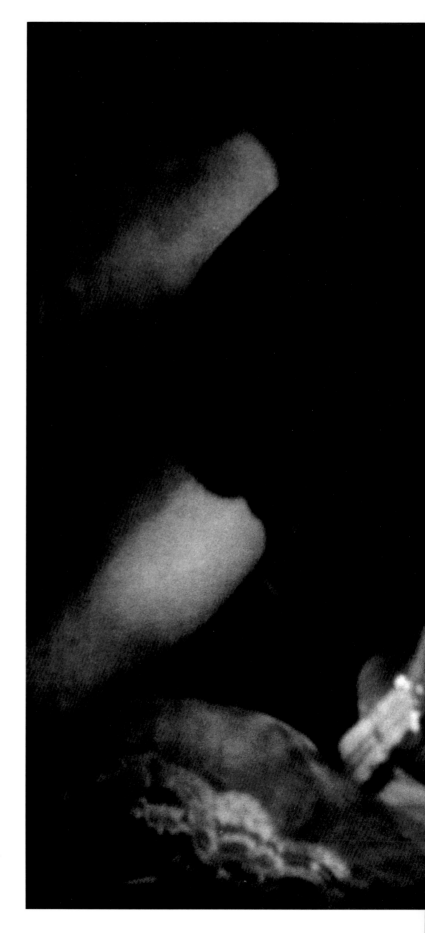

"We've had this rendezvous with each other from the very first day." During the shooting of A Streetcar Named Desire, *Alfred Eisenstaedt shot the scene in which Stanley rapes Blanche, 1951.*

Scene from A Streetcar Named Desire, *1951.*

In the famous reconciliation scene, Stella walks slowly down the stairs toward Stanley.
The shot of Brando's bare back and torn T shirt became the movie's hallmark.
Scene from A Streetcar Named Desire, *1951.*

Marlon Brando with Vivien Leigh during a pause in the shooting of A
Streetcar Named Desire. *Brando thought the choice of Vivien Leigh
was "perfect casting. In many ways she was Blanche. She was
memorably beautiful, one of the great beauties of the screen, but she
was also vulnerable, and her own life had been very much like that of
Tennessee's wounded butterfly. It had paralleled Blanche's in several
ways, especially when her mind began to wobble and her sense of self
became vague. Like Blanche, she slept with almost everybody ..."*

Marlon Brando as the Mexican revolutionary
Emiliano Zapata, in Elia Kazan's movie Viva Zapata!,
photographed by Alfred Eisenstaedt, 1952.

Scene from Viva Zapata!, *1952. On his wedding night, Emiliano (Marlon Brando) asks Josefa (Jean Peters) to teach him how to read.*

Scene from Viva Zapata!, *1952.*
Brando as Zapata and Jean Peters in the part of Josefa.

After his role as a Mexican revolutionary hero, Brando slips into the classic role
of Mark Antony in Joseph L. Mankiewicz's version of Julius Caesar. *Still by John Swope,*
with Brando and Louis Calhern, who played Caesar, 1953.

Close-up of Brando during Mark Antony's great funeral oration after Caesar's murder.
Still by John Swope from Julius Caesar, *1953.*

Brando hardly prepared for any of his roles in a more disciplined way than he did for Mark Antony. He performed the famous speech, the climax of Shakespeare's drama, several times, so that the camera and the cutters would be able to make as much of it as possible. An American intruding into the domain of British theatre, he received the 1953 British Film Academy Award for his acting in Julius Caesar.

With *The Wild One*, in which Brando plays Johnny, the young leader of a band of motorcycle gangsters terrorizing a small town, Hollywood took up for the first time in 1963 the theme of the approaching generation clash and young gang crime. Brando, who had been a rebel against every form of authority since his childhood, summed the movie up as heralding the worldwide revolution of youth: "There's a line in the picture where he snarls, 'Nobody tells *me* what to do.' That's exactly how I've felt all my life."

Still from The Wild One, *1953.*

Still from The Wild One, *1953, with Johnny (Brando), two of his buddies, and Kathie,
the daughter of the sheriff and bar-owner, played by Mary Murphy.
Through his attraction to and self-sacrifice for Kathie, the audience is finally reconciled
to the rebel Johnny after all.*

*Sales of motorbikes and black leather jackets skyrocketed after the première
of* The Wild One. *This still of Brando became an artistic icon of the twentieth century
when Andy Warhol used it as the basis for one of his famous screenprint series (right).*

Scene with Brando and Mary Murphy from The Wild One, *1953.*

Still from The Wild One, *1953.*

"A young world star with his aging parents," could be the caption for this picture taken when Brando's parents visited him on location during the shooting of On the Waterfront *in Hoboken, New Jersey, in December 1953. Brando's relationship with his parents was a difficult one. For his mother, a musically talented woman who suffered from alcoholism, he had a touching affection that was plagued, however, by strong feelings of guilt. His relationship with his father seems to have been marked more by a mixture of rebellion and submissiveness. Brando had bought his parents a ranch in southern Nebarska with his acting fees. When this photo was taken, Dorothy Brando, smiling into the camera here between her husband and her son, had only a few months left to live.*

73

On the Waterfront *is a story of corruption and terror on the docks.*
Elia Kazan hired Marlon Brando to play Terry Malloy, who is caught in a conflict between apparent loyalty
and alleged betrayal. Still by Elliott Erwitt from On the Waterfront, *1954.*

Still from On the Waterfront, *1954.*

In his autobiography, director Elia Kazan wrote, "If there is a better performance by a man in the history of film in America, I don't know what it is." Still from On the Waterfront, *with Marlon Brando as Terry Malloy, 1954.*

Scene from On the Waterfront *with Brando in the role of Terry Malloy and his co-star, Eva Maria Saint, as Edie Doyle. Elia Kazan later repeatedly said that, for him, the love scenes between the two were the best part of the movie.*

Désirée, in which Brando plays Napoleon, was a compensation for Darryl Zanuck of Fox,
to whom Brando owed a second big movie through his contract for Viva Zapata!.
In Brando's eyes, Désirée was a "superficial and dismal" movie.
"I was astonished when told it had been a success." 1954.

Brando recalled Jean Simmons, who co-starred in the picture as Désirée: "She was winning, charming, beautiful and experienced, and we had fun together. Unfortunately, she was married to Stewart Granger, the great white hunter." Scene from Désirée, *1954.*

Marilyn Monroe visiting the set of Désirée. *When the photo was taken, Marilyn and Brando had already been the closest of friends for several years. 1954.*

When the successful Broadway musical Guys and Dolls *was turned into a movie in 1955, Brando had to learn how to sing and dance. Bob Willoughby took this photo of Brando on the phone during a break in the dancing.*

Brando as Sky Masterson and Jean Simmons in the part of Sarah Brown. Still from Guys and Dolls, *1955.*

During the shooting of Guys and Dolls, *Brando visited Elia Kazan on the set of his new movie project,* East of Eden, *in which James Dean had his first leading part. James Dean admired Brando and was always tempted to imitate him. Or at least, that was how Brando and some of the public saw it. The fact that the obvious similarities might have their origin in the personality of their common director, Elia Kazan, was mostly overlooked.*

From left to right: Elia Kazan, Marlon Brando, Julie Harris, James Dean.

Marlon Brando and Miiko Tara in a scene from Sayonara, *1957.*
During the shooting in Kyoto, Brando gave a long interview to the writer Truman Capote,
based on which Capote wrote his much-admired literary portrait of the actor.
The interview is reprinted as the introduction to the present book.

The movie *The Young Lions* was shot in 1957 in Europe, mainly in Paris and Berlin. It is the story of three young soldiers, two Americans (Montgomery Clift as the Jew, Noah Ackerman, and Dean Martin as Michael Whiteacre, a showbusiness entrepreneur) and a German (Marlon Brando as Christian Diestl), whose paths cross during the Second World War.

Brando's interpretation of the German, Christian Diestl, led to a severe dispute with the writer, Irwin Shaw, who had written the novel under the influence of wartime hatred for the Germans, while Brando twelve years after the war gave Diestl a character that develops and recognizes the horror. At a press conference in Berlin, Brando said, "The picture will try to show that Nazism is a matter of mind, not geography, and that there are Nazis—and people of good will—in every country. The world can't spend its life looking over its shoulder and nursing hatreds. There would be no progress that way." A German journalist commented, "Brando speaks more like a statesman than an movie actor."

Marlon Brando as Christian Diestl, who to begin with feels like a "young, golden god of war,"
as he is called in the movie.

95

Marlon Brando and May Britt as
Gretchen Hardenburg in The Young Lions, *1958.*

Still from The Young Lions, *1958.*

The Fugitive Kind was the movie version of Tennessee William's play *Orpheus Descending*. Brando played the vagabond Val Xavier, who gets involved with an older woman—played by Anna Magnani—in a small town in Missouri. The director was Sidney Lumet.

The still shows a scene with the two main actors, Magnani and Brando, 1960.

Still from The Fugitive Kind, *with Anna Magnani and Marlon Brando, 1960.*

Still from The Fugitive Kind, *with Anna Magnani and Marlon Brando, 1960.*

Still from The Fugitive Kind, *1960.*

One-Eyed Jacks was the first movie by Brando's own production company, Pennebaker Productions. The script of the Western was based on the novel *The Authentic Death of Henry Jones,* by Charles Neider. When Brando failed to find a director for the film—Stanley Kubrick, Elia Kazan, and Sidney Lumet all declined—he felt forced to take on the directing himself, in addition to playing the central role. During the shooting, he lost the thread: "I didn't know what I was doing. I was making things up by the moment, not sure where the story was going." The film overran its shooting time and budget by nearly a hundred percent, and cured Brando of any desire to direct again. He didn't even have any interest in the cutting of the six to eight hours of film that were shot.

Still from One-Eyed Jacks, *1960.*

Still from One-Eyed Jacks, *1960.*

*One-Eyed Jacks was shot in Death Valley, on the coast of California at Big Sur,
and on the Monterey peninsula. The film includes impressive individual performances and
outstanding landscape shots. Still with Brando as the bandit Rio, 1960.*

Brando (Rio) and Pina Pellicer (Louisa). Still from One-Eyed Jacks, *1960.*

Faced with the choice to shoot *Lawrence of Arabia* in the desert or do a remake of *Mutiny on the Bounty* in Tahiti, Brando at once opted for Tahiti, which had been the land of his dreams ever since his school days. For a moment, dream and reality not only seemed to coincide, but reality even seemed to be better than any dream. "I had some of the best times of my life making *Mutiny on the Bounty,* Brando wrote. He tried to hold on to this happiness. The female lead, Taritatumi Teriipaia, became his partner, and they were to have two children. Brando bought the coral atoll of Teti'aroa near Tahiti. Today he still divides his time between Beverly Hills and Teti'aroa.

Still from Mutiny on the Bounty, *1962.*

Still from Mutiny on the Bounty, *1962.*

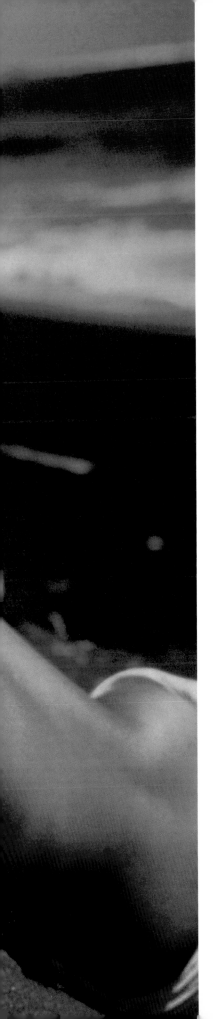

Still from Mutiny on the Bounty,
showing Marlon Brando on the beach in Tahiti with his
future partner, Taritatumi Teriipaia, 1962.

Still from Bedtime Story, 1964, *a gangster comedy set on the Riviera.*
Brando's fellow gangster in the movie was David Niven.

Still from The Chase, *directed by Arthur Penn, 1966. In addition to Brando,
the movie featured Jane Fonda and Robert Redford in his first big part,
as well as Brando's sister Jocelyn in a minor role.*

*Brando as Sheriff Calder in a shot taken by William Claxton
during the shooting of* The Chase, *1965 (left).*

Still from The Chase, *1966.*
On the left, Brando as Sheriff Calder,
and Robert Redford on the right
as Bubber Reeves.

Marlon Brando as Matt.
Still from The Appaloosa, *1966.*

Marlon Brando and his co-star Anjanette Comer.
Still from The Appaloosa, *1966.*

Brando recalled the shooting of Charlie Chaplin's late work *A Countess from Hong Kong* in 1966 as one of his disasters. The aging Chaplin struck Brando as "probably the most sadistic man I'd ever met." Sophia Loren played Natasha, an impoverished dancer, who stows away in Brando's cabin on a luxury liner. In his memoirs, Brando does not mention Sophia Loren once. Charlie Chaplin is reported to have had to remind the couple again and again that the movie was supposed to be a love story.

Still from A Countess from Hong Kong, *1966.*

Still from A Countess from Hong Kong, *1966.*

Brando as the diplomat Ogden and Charlie Chaplin, who not only directed
but also played the ship's steward.

Still from Reflections in a Golden Eye, *1967. In the movie, Brando plays a frustrated major who is trying to repress his homosexuality. Brando's appearance in the film is more likely to have been one of his famous efforts to make money rather than a matter of genuine concern.*

After a series of expensive flops during the sixties, which was not really Brando's decade, at the beginning of the seventies he came back into fashion with a masterpiece that outdid even the ecstatic beginnings of his acting career in the early fifties. In Francis Ford Coppola's *The Godfather,* he plays Don Corleone, the head of an American Mafia family. Mario Puzo, author of the novel as well as the script for the film, suggested Brando for the part. One problem was age, since Brando at forty-seven had to play an Italian who at the beginning of the story is fifty and at the end of it seventy-five. Brando had his doubts, but was full of determination: "I went home and did some rehearsing to satisfy my curiosity about whether I could play an Italian. I put on some makeup, stuffed Kleenex in my cheeks, and worked out the characterization first in front of a mirror, then on a television monitor. After working on it, I decided I could create a characterization that would support the story. The people at Paramount saw the footage and liked it, and that's how I became the Godfather."

Marlon Brando as Don Corleone. Still from The Godfather, *1971.*

Marlon Brando built up the character of Don Corleone in quite a positive way: "I had a great deal of respect for Don Corleone; I saw him as a man of substance, tradition, dignity, refinement, a man of unerring instinct who just happened to live in a violent world and who had to protect himself and his family in this environment."
Still from The Godfather, *1971.*

Don Corleone and his son Michael, played by Al Pacino.
Still from The Godfather, *1971.*

Brando's biographer Jörg Fauser sees the Brando–Coppola duo as being
"a magnificent romantic study of the mentality of violence and the politics of crime."
Still from The Godfather, *1971.*

Don Corleone and his grandson in the famous garden scene,
in which a heart attack brings the Godfather's life to an end.
Still from The Godfather, *1971.*

The shooting of *The Godfather* was hardly over before Brando started on *Last Tango in Paris,* directed by Bernardo Bertolucci. He plays a newly widowed American who starts an affair in Paris with a girl from a good background. When it became known that the film was to include permissive sex scenes—Brando had agreed to do these for the first time in his career—the media were gripped, even in advance of the film's release, by a fever of the sort that only Madonna at her best would later be able to evoke.

Bertolucci suspected that Brando's personality alone would be enough to transform the film from a piece of raw sexual exhibitionism à la Warhol into a film for a wide audience. He told Brando to play himself, and gave him a partner in Maria Schneider who did not inhibit him in any way. Brando commented, "He wanted me to play myself, to improvise completely and portray Paul as if he were an autobiographical mirror of me . . . he had me write virtually all my scenes and dialogue." In his memoirs, Brando claims that even today he doesn't know what the film is really about.

Still of Marlon Brando as Paul in Last Tango in Paris, *1972.*

Still from Last Tango in Paris, *1972.*

*Brando with his film partner, Maria Schneider. Bertolucci
selected the unknown actress on the spur of the moment in
Paris from more than fifty candidates. "A superb example of
the narcissistic hysterics of the hippie generation," is Jörg
Fauser's description of her. But Bertolucci saw her rather
differently: "A Lolita—only much more perverse."
Still from* Last Tango in Paris, *1972.*

Still from Last Tango in Paris, *1972.*

Still from Last Tango in Paris, *1972.*

Still from Last Tango in Paris, *1972.*

Still from Last Tango in Paris, *1972.*

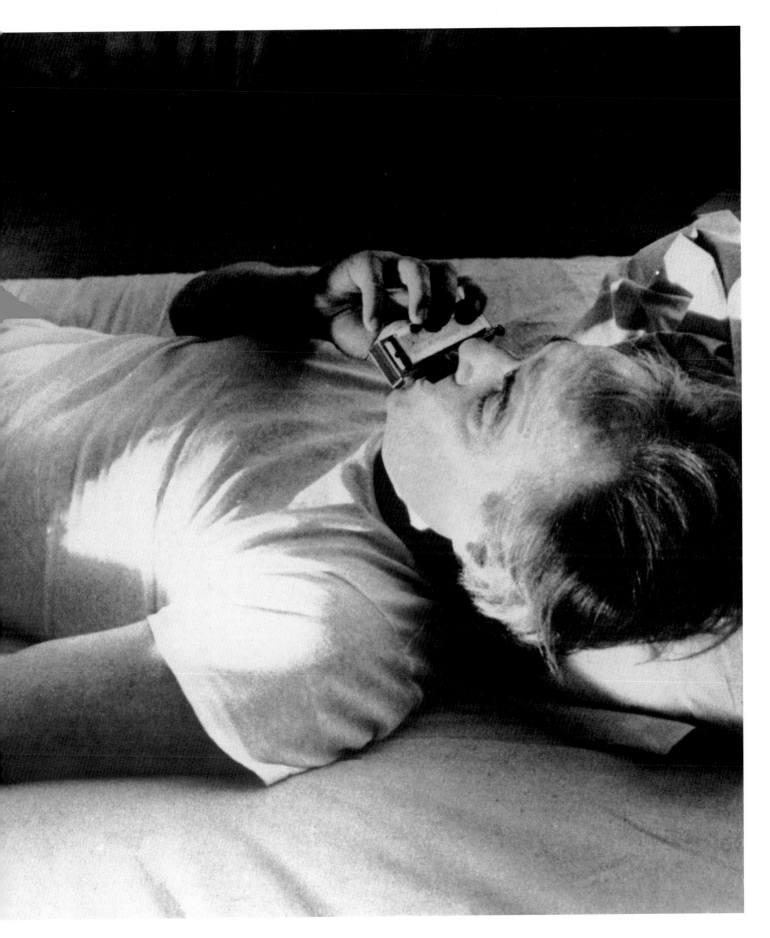

Bertolucci knew he would be able to rely on the greatness of a star, and praised him in the highest tones: "He has the wisdom of an ancient Indian. Like a figure painted by Bacon, everything that comes out of his inner being bears a facial expression that has the same rugged plasticity. The Tibetan quality in his character and his physical presence is extraordinary."

Still from Last Tango in Paris, *1972.*

In The Missouri Breaks, *Brando plays
the sadistic killer Robert Lee Clayton.
Still from* The Missouri Breaks, *1976.*

Still from The Missouri Breaks, *1976.*

The killer sometimes turns up as a transvestite. Photo by Mary Ellen Mark
during the shooting of The Missouri Breaks, *1976.*

The figure of Major Kurtz, played by Brando in *Apocalypse Now*, is based on Joseph Conrad's novel *Heart of Darkness*. Conrad depicts Kurtz as "impressively bald," so Brando prompty shaved his head. His transformation into a negative Buddha was an immediate success.

Photo by Mary Ellen Mark, taken during the shooting of Apocalypse Now
in the Philippines, 1979.

Still from Apocalypse Now, *1979.*

*"I wrote Kurtz's speeches, including a monologue at his death that must have been forty-five minutes long.
It was probably the closest I've ever come to getting lost in a part ... I made it up extremporaneously,
bringing up images like a snail crawling along the edge of a razor. I was hysterical;
I cried and laughed, and it was a wonderful scene."*
Still from Apocalypse Now, *1979 (right).*

After a pause of almost ten years, Brando was in front of the camera once more in 1990,
giving a parody of his Godfather *in* The Freshman.

Brando's latest prank is his portrayal of the New York police psychiatrist Jack Mickler, in *Don Juan DeMarco,* whose job it is to cure Johnny Depp of his Don Juan mania. However, Mickler lets his patient's sex-crazed stories inspire him so much that his own marriage becomes sexually rekindled. With his decades of experience on various psychiatrist's couches and his many wild erotic adventures, Brando is superbly qualified for the part.

Still from Don Juan DeMarco, *1995.*

Brando as the psychiatrist Mickler, with his wife, played by Faye Dunaway, after the sexual renaissance of their marriage. Still from Don Juan DeMarco, *1995*

Biography

On 3 April 1924, Marlon Brando is born in Omaha, Nebraska, the third and last child of Dorothy Pennebaker-Brando and Marlon Brando, Senior. The family, with his sisters Jocelyn and Frances, then five and two years old, respectively, has been living in Nebraska for generations, and is descended from Irish immigrants.

Brando Senior earns his living as a traveling salesman for construction materials and animal foodstuff. His relationship to his growing son is an extremely distanced one. "Nothing I did ever pleased or even interested him ... I don't remember him being affectionate with anybody except maybe our dogs," was Brando's disillusioned verdict in later years.

His mother, whom Brando described as a "delicate, funny woman who loved music and learning," is an alcoholic, and she often neglects the children. (In her youth she had been one of the founders of the "Omaha Community Playhouse," an amateur theatre group with very high standards that became well known later on.) When their nanny Ermit leaves the family to get married, the boy is devastated. "From that day forward, I became estranged from this world."

1930 The family moves to Evanston, Illinois, a small university town near Chicago, where Brando Senior starts his own company. Marlon, now six, reacts to domestic problems with bad school results and general resistance to authority, and begins to stutter.

1935 The parents separate, and their mother moves with the three children to Santa Ana in Orange County, California, where their grandparents live. Marlon is eleven. "My mother drank more than ever," and "In Santa Ana, I had a fantasy that the important people in my life were all dead and were only pretending to be alive," Brando later recalled.

1937 Their parents are reconciled again, and the family moves to Libertyville, Illinois, north of Chicago near Lake Michigan. "Once again, we all looked forward to a fresh start." Instead, however, things go on as usual. "I used to come home from school and nobody would be home. There would be dirty dishes in the sink and piles of cat turds under the piano. The beds weren't made, and the whole house would be unkept and empty. My sisters were either still at school or with friends, my mother was out drinking and my father was out whoring. ... I have many pleasant memories of my childhood, however."

Brando's school results are increasingly poor. He resists all forms of authority and often plays truant.

1940 His father takes him away from Libertyville High School and sends him to a military boarding school, Shattuck Military Academy in Faribault, Minnesota. "I was sixteen when I arrived at Shattuck. ... My tenure at Shattuck was probably fated from the beginning to be short. By then I was rebelling against any authority and against conformity in general with every ounce of energy in my body." The only bright spot for him in Shattuck is a teacher by the name of Earl Wagner, nicknamed "Duke," who not only teaches English but also runs the boarding school's drama group. He arouses an enthusiasm for Shakespeare in Brando, and gives him a part in a play. Brando's performance turns out to be the seventeen-year-old's first, much longed for, experience of success. "When my friends said that I had done well and Duke did too, I felt good. Except for sports, it was the first time since my shop teacher at Julius C. Lathrop Junior High in Santa Ana had said he liked my work that anyone had ever told me I did anything well."

When Brando is finally expelled from the school for insubordination, Earl Wagner encourages him by saying, "Don't worry, Marlon, everything will be all right. I know the world is going to hear from you."

Brando returns to his parents' home in Libertyville, and to begin with takes on a job as a building worker. Then he decides (America has by this time joined the Second World War) to enlist in the Army. But this powerful institution, too, rejects the young man: due to a knee injury, he is classed as unfit for service and dismissed.

After an odyssey through America's institutions of learning that had ended with so little distinction, Brando makes a highly realistic assessment of his chances: "Since the only thing I had ever done except sports that anyone had praised me for was acting, I told them, 'Why don't I go to New York and try to be an actor?'"

In spring 1943, the nineteen-year-old arrives in New York, where he first moves into his sisters' apartment in Greenwich Village; they are studying acting and painting in the city.

In the fall, while earning his living from temporary jobs, he enrolls in a course at the Dramatic Workshop of the New School for Social Research, directed by the German emigrant Erwin Piscator. His teacher at the Dramatic Workshop is Stella Adler, who for Brando is the "soul" of the school. Stella Adler had lived in Moscow in the early 1930s, and had studied with Konstantin Stanislavsky at the Moscow Arts Theatre. On returning to America, she taught the members of the left-wing Group Theatre using Stanislavsky's "method," according to which actors have to develop every part they play out of the emotions of their own personality—a method also later taught by Lee Strasberg, from whom Brando explicitly distances himself, however: "Strasberg never taught me anything. Stella did— and later Kazan." Stella Adler's training focused on developing a talent for precise observation and the actor's own imagination, an approach that is ideally suited to Brando's natural gifts. Years later, she says, "He's the most keenly aware, the most empathetical human being alive. . . . He just knows. If you have a scar, physical or mental, he goes right to it. He doesn't want to, but he doesn't avoid it. . . . He cannot be cheated or fooled. If you left the room he could be you."

In 1944 Brando has his stage debut at the Dramatic Workshops as Jesus in Gerhart Hauptmann's play *Hannele.*

Roles in Molière's *Malade imaginaire* and Shakespeare's *As You Like It* follow. When Piscator discovers Brando in a haystack with a girl during a summer performance by the group, he dismisses him. It is a stroke of luck, as it turns out. Three weeks after his dismissal, the twenty-year-old Brando gets his first engagement with the Rodgers and Hammerstein Broadway production of *I Remember Mama,* by John Van Druten. The play premières on 19 October 1944, and is so successful that it runs for two years. This means that Brando is for the first time finally free of any financial worries. However, the play's long run leads to problems of physical and mental fatigue.

Brando falls into a severe mental crisis, caused by the fact that his mother, who left her husband at the end of 1943 and moved to New York to be with her children, had another reconciliation with his father and returned to Libertyville. Brando sees this as a personal failure on his own part, and suffers from feelings of guilt over it for a long time: "I'd had another chance to offer her my love, which I did, but it wasn't enough for her."

Brando is now being represented by theatre agent Edith von Cleve.

In the spring of 1946, Brando plays in Maxwell Anderson's *Truckline Café,* then in George Bernard Shaw's *Candida,* and in the fall of the same years has a part in *A Flag Is Born,* a play by Ben Hecht with music by Kurt Weill, about the founding of the state of Israel. "The play, as well as my friendship with the Adlers, helped make me a zealous advocate for Israel." Powerfully impressed by the reports and pictures of Nazi concentration camps, he joins the American League for a Free Palestine, and collects money for the radical Jewish underground movement Irgun Zwai Lemi.

This first experience of political commitment is a first sign of the pattern of his spontaneous expression of his sense of justice, which is later to lead to his lifelong commitment to the political rights of the American Indians.

1947 Brando's great moment is approaching, when Elia Kazan suggests him for the part of Stanley Kowalski in Tennessee Williams's *A Streetcar Named Desire.* After auditioning with Tennessee Williams, he is given the part. He triumphantly writes to his father, "I start rehearsals on Oct. 4th [1947] for a 'Streetcar Named Desire.' I'm getting $550 [a week] and second billing. Elia Kazan is directing." The Broadway première on December 1947 is a sensational success, and overnight Brando becomes a star celebrated by audiences and critics alike. But success also has side-effects—good and bad: "What I remember most about *A Streetcar Named Desire* was the emotional grind of acting in it six nights and two afternoons a week … it was emotionally draining, wearisome, and after a few weeks I wanted out of it," and "I hated going to work."

A more pleasant side of it was the sexual paradise that opened up to the young man in the wake of his professional success. Without the slightest hesitation, the mama boy became transformed into a materialist: "Every night after the performance, there would be seven or eight girls waiting in my dressing room. I looked them over and chose one for the night. For a twenty-four-year-old who was eager to follow his penis wherever it could go, it was wonderful." The drudgery of the work was to last for almost two years and 855 performances.

In 1949, when *A Streetcar Named Desire* closed after a two-year run, Brando went on a three-month tour of Europe. Most of the time he stayed in Paris, where he led a life of pleasure: "Anything that was imaginable, I did in Paris. When I returned to New York, most of my clothes and almost everything I owned were gone."

And when Brando says "Anything that was imaginable," there is not the slightest reason to doubt him.

In 1950, Brando turns his back on Broadway and goes to Hollywood, since he sees the movies as being a way of earning more money with less work, while reaching a wider audience than was possible in the theatre. He is never to return to the stage.

When the Korean War breaks out, Brando is called up again. When he answers a question about his race by saying "human," and about his color of skin by saying "Seasonal—oyster white to beige," he is rejected as unsuitable for military service, as he is undergoing psychiatric treatment and has already been dismissed from a military school.

In the five years from *1950 to 1955,* Brando has the leading part in eight films, all of which become world hits: *The Men* (1950), *A Streetcar Named Desire* (1951), *Viva Zapata!* (1952), *Julius Caesar* (1953), *The Wild One* (1953), *On the Waterfront* (1954), *Desirée* (1954), and *Guys and Dolls* (1955).

After this, he is considered to be one of the greatest actors of his generation, if not in history. Director Elia Kazan described him as "the only genius I have ever met in the field of acting." Tennessee Williams said, "I think he is probably the greatest living actor," and suspects that Brando's comet-like ascent was one reason for the "long and dreadful crack up of dear Monty [Montgomery Clift]."

On 31 March 1954, three days before Brando's thirtieth birthday, his mother dies at the age of 57.

In the spring of 1955, Brando founds his own production company, calling it "Pennebaker Productions," after his mother's maiden name. His three aims in starting the company are "To make films that promote the good things in the world; to give my father a job that would keep him busy after my mother's death; and to save taxes."

In 1955, Brando receives his first Oscar (having been nominated on three previous occasions) for his part as Terry Malloy in *On the Waterfront.* "If I regretted anything, it may have been that Duke Wagner wasn't around for that evening. By that time he was dead."

During the shooting of *Sayonara,* Brando gives a long interview in Kyoto to the writer Truman Capote, on which Capote bases a literary portrait of the actor that is published in the *New Yorker.* Brando is so disturbed by the essay that he refuses to give any interviews again.

On 11 October 1957, he marries the actress Anna Kashfi, from Wales. The marriage produces a son, Christian Devi. Later Marlon Brando will state in court that his sole reason for marrying Anna Kashfi was the fact that she was pregnant. He will also describe her as the "most destructive and brutal person I have ever met." When they are divorced on *22 August 1959,* the dispute over custody of their son Christian Devi keeps the courts busy for a further twelve years.

His second marriage is to the Mexican actress Movita Castaneda, in 1960, divorce following in 1968. From this marriage he has two children, Simon and Rebecca.

1960 During the shooting of *Mutiny on the Bounty* in Tahiti—"I had some of the best times of my life making *Mutiny on the Bounty*"—he discovers the coral atoll Teti'aroa, which he will purchase in 1966. After 1966, Brando divides his time between Beverly Hills and the island. His relationship with the Tahitian Taritatumi Teriipaia, his co-star in the filming of the *Bounty,* produces two more children, his son Teikuto and his daughter Cheyenne.

In the spring of 1965, his father, with whom Brando had a love-hate relationship, dies.

During the 1960s, movie-making becomes more and more just a means of making a lot of money with as little work as possible for Brando. He describes this functional attitude to his talent extremely soberly and without ambitiousness: "Having had the luck to be successful as an actor also afforded me the luxury of time. I only had to do a movie once a year, for three months at the most, which paid me enough so that I didn't have to work again until my business manager called and said, 'We've got to pay your taxes at the end of the year, so you'd better make another movie.' When that happened, I'd look around and grab something."

He also attempts to make a contribution toward ending racial discrimination and social injustice by involving himself in the 1960s Civil Rights Movement. His commitment above all is to improving the miserable conditions of the American Indians: "When the Indian civil rights movement grew and became more important in the late sixties and early seventies, I supported it in every way I could—emotionally, intellectually, and financially."

With his portrayal of Don Corleone in *The Godfather,* Brando enjoys a tremendous artistic comeback, which Hollywood had thought him incapable of, and receives an Oscar for the best actor of *1972.*

Brando has an Indian, Sacheen Littlefeather, represent him at the Oscar ceremony on 27 March 1973, and she makes the following declaration: "To his great regret, Marlon Brando feels unable to accept this award. The reasons lie in the treatment of the Indian in TV and the movies in this country, and in the recent events at Wounded Knee."

The longer version of Brando's declaration, which Sacheen Littlefeather is unable to read out as she is only allotted 45 seconds, is still well worth reading: "For 200 years we have said to the Indian people who are fighting for their land, their life, their families and their right to be free, 'Lay down your arms, my friends, and then we will remain together. Only if you lay down your arms, my friends, can we then talk of peace and come to an agreement which will be good for you.' When they laid down their arms, we murdered them. We lied to them, we cheated them out of their lands. We starved them into signing fraudulent agreements that we call treaties that we never kept. We turned them into beggars on a continent that gave them life for as long as life can remember. And by my interpretation of history, however twisted, we did not do right. ... Perhaps at this moment you are saying to yourselves, what the hell does all this have to do with the Academy Awards? Why is this woman standing up here ruining our evening, invading our lives with things that don't concern us and that we don't care about. Wasting our time and money and intruding in our homes. I think the answer to those unspoken questions is that the motion picture community has been as responsible as any for degrading the Indian and making a mockery of his character ... as a member of this profession, [I] do not feel that I can as a citizen of the United States accept an award here tonight. I think awards in this country at this time are inappropriate to be received or given until the condition of the American Indian is drastically altered. If we are not our brother's keeper, at least let us not be his executioner."

Two more movies follow *The Godfather* during the 1970s, in which Brando signalizes his return not only as a top earner but also as a man at the peak of the art of movie acting: in 1972, in the principal part in *Last Tango in Paris,* and in 1979, in his brief appearance as Major Kurtz in *Apocalypse Now.* A pause of nearly a decade then follows. "In the ten years between *The Formula* (1980) and *The Freshman* (1990), I didn't make a single movie apart from *A Dry White Season* (1989), because I didn't need any money."

Brando succeeds in keeping out of the public eye for almost ten years. It had always been important to him to keep information about his family private. He lives secluded with his nine children (including several adopted children), and spends a great deal of time on his island. A hotel project on the atoll falls through. He does a lot of reading, and shows an interest in the problems of tropical agriculture and alternative energy projects. He also founds a research station for marine biology.

On 16 May 1990, a terrible family tragedy takes place in Brando's house on Mulholland Drive in Beverly Hills. Following an argument, Brando's 32-year-old son Christian Devi shoots dead Dag Drollet, the lover—and father of the future child—of his sister Cheyenne. After a spectacular trial, during which Brando testifies as a witness to the crime and as the father, Christian Devi Brando is sentenced by a court in Santa Monica to ten years in jail for homicide. When Dag Drollet's parents bring charges against Cheyenne in Tahiti for acting as an accessory to murder, Cheyenne makes two suicide attempts.

The charges are dismissed by the court in Papeete. However, Cheyenne Brando, deeply depressed, takes her own life in 1994.

In the same year, Brando's sister Frances dies.

On 3 April 1994, Marlon Brando turns seventy.

In the fall of 1994, Brando publishes his autobiography. He receives an advance of five million dollars for the book, which is dedicated to his sisters, his children, his psychoanalyst, an Indian friend, and a young member of the Black Panther movement who was shot dead by the police.

Filmography

1 THE MEN
Director: Fred Zinnemann; script: Carl Foreman; camera: Robert de Grasse; cast: Marlon Brando (Ken), Teresa Wright (Ellen), Everett Sloan (Dr. Brock), Jack Webb (Norm), Richard Erdman (Leo), and others; length: 85 minutes; production and distribution: Stanley Kramer / United Artists; première: 1950.

2 A STREETCAR NAMED DESIRE
Director: Elia Kazan; script: Tennessee Williams, after his play; camera: Harry Stradling; cast: Vivien Leigh (Blanche), Marlon Brando (Stanley Kowalski), Kim Hunter (Stella Kowalski), Karl Malden (Mitch), Rudy Bond (Steve), and others; length: 122 minutes; production and distribution: Charles K. Feldman / Warner Bros.; première: 1951.

3 VIVA ZAPATA!
Director: Elia Kazan; script: John Steinbeck; camera: Joe MacDonald; cast: Marlon Brando (Zapata), Jean Peters (Josefa), Anthony Quinn (Eufemio), Joseph Wiseman (Fernando), Arnold Moss (Don Nacio), Alan Reed (Pancho Villa), and others; length: 113 minutes; production and distribution: Twentieth Century-Fox, Darryl F. Zanuck; première: 1952.

4 JULIUS CAESAR
Director: Joseph L. Mankiewicz; script: Joseph L. Mankiewicz, after the play by William Shakespeare; camera: Joseph Ruttenberg; cast: Louis Calhern (Julius Caesar), Marlon Brando (Mark Anton), James Mason (Brutus), John Gielgud (Cassius), Greer Garson (Calpurnia), Deborah Kerr (Portia), Edmond O'Brian (Casca), and others; length: 121 minutes; production and distribution: John Houseman / MGM; première: 1953.

5 THE WILD ONE
Director: Laslo Benedek; script: John Paxton, after a story by Frank Rooney; camera: Hal Mohr; cast: Marlon Brando (Johnny), Mary Murphy (Kathie), Robert Keith (Harry Bleeker), Lee Marvin (Chino), Jay C. Flippen (Sheriff Singer), and others; length: 79 minutes; production and distribution: Stanley Kramer / Columbia Pictures; première: 1953.

6 ON THE WATERFRONT
Director: Elia Kazan; script: Budd Schulberg, after articles by Malcolm Johnson; camera: Boris Kaufman; cast: Marlon Brando (Terry Malloy), Eva Marie Saint (Edie Doyle), Karl Malden (Father Barry), Lee J. Cobb (Johnny Friendly), Rod Steiger (Charley Malloy), Pat Henning (Kayo Dugan), Leif Erickson (Gover), John Hamilton (Pop Doyle), and others; length: 108 minutes; production and distribution: Sam Spiegel / Columbia Pictures; première: 1954.

7 DESIRÉE
Director: Henry Koster; script: Daniel Taradash, after a novel by Annemarie Selinko; camera: Milton Krasner; cast: Jean Simmons (Desirée), Marlon Brando (Napoleon), Merle Oberon (Joséphine), Michael Rennie (Bernadotte), Cameron Mitchell (Joseph Bonaparte), Elizabeth Sellars (Julie), and others; length: 110 minutes; production and distribution: Twentieth Century-Fox, Julian Blaustein; première: 1954.

8   GUYS AND DOLLS
Director: Joseph L. Mankiewicz; script: Joseph L. Mankiewicz, after the musical by Jo Swerling und Abe Burrows; camera: Harry Stradling; cast: Marlon Brando (Sky Masterson), Jean Simmons (Sarah Brown), Frank Sinatra (Nathan Detroit), Vivian Blaine (Miss Adelaide), Stubby Kaye (Nicely-Nicely Johnson), Robert Keith (Lieutenant Brannigan), and others; length: 149 minutes; production and distribution: Samuel Goldwyn/MGM; première: 1955.

9   THE TEAHOUSE OF THE AUGUST MOON
Director: Daniel Mann; script: John Patrick, after his play and the novel by Vern J. Sneider; camera: John Alton; cast: Marlon Brando (Sakini), Glenn Ford (Captain Fisby), Machiko Kyo (Lotus Blossom), Eddie Albert (Captain McLean), Paul Ford (Colonel Purdy), and others; length: 123 minutes; production and distribution: MGM, Jack Cummings; première: 1956.

10   SAYONARA
Director: Joshua Logan; script: Paul Osborn, after the novel by James A. Michener; camera: Ellsworth Fredericks; cast: Marlon Brando (Major Lloyd Gruver), Miiko Taka (Hana-Ogi), Patricia Owens (Eileen Webster), Red Buttons (Kelly), Miyoshi Umeki (Katsumi), James Garner (Bailey), and others; length: 147 minutes; production and distribution: William Goetz/Warner Bros.; première: 1957.

11   THE YOUNG LIONS
Director: Edward Dmytryk; script: Edward Anhalt, after a novel by Irwin Shaw; camera: Joe MacDonald; cast: Marlon Brando (Christian Diestl), Montgomery Clift (Noah Ackerman), Dean Martin (Michael Whiteacre), Hope Lange (Hope Plowman), Barbara Rush (Margaret Freemantle), May Britt (Gretchen Hardenburg), Maximilian Schell (Hardenburg), Dora Doll (Simone), Lee Van Cleef (Sergeant Rickett), and others; length: 167 minutes; production and distribution: Al Lichtman, Twentieth Century-Fox; première: 1958.

12   THE FUGITIVE KIND
Director: Sidney Lumet; script: Tennessee Williams and Reade Roberts, after the play *Orpheus descending* by Tennessee Williams; camera: Boris Kaufman; cast: Marlon Brando (Val Xavier), Anna Magnani (Lady Torrance), Joanne Woodward (Carol Cutrere), Victor Jory (Jabe Torrance), and others; length: 119 minutes; production and distribution: Martin Jurow, Richard A. Shepherd (Pennebaker)/United Artists; première: 1960.

13   ONE-EYED JACKS
Director: Marlon Brando; script: Guy Trosper and Calder Willingham, after the novel *The Authentic Death of Hendry Jones* by Charles Neider; camera: Charles Lang Jr.; cast: Marlon Brando (Rio), Karl Malden (Dad Longworth), Pina Pellicer (Louisa), Katy Jurado (Maria), Ben Johnson (Bob Amory), Slim Pickens (Lon), Larry Duran (Modesto), Sam Gilman (Harvey Johnson), and others; length: 141 minutes; production and distribution: Frank P. Rosenberg, Pennebaker/Paramount Pictures; première: 1960.

14   MUTINY ON THE BOUNTY
Director: Lewis Milestone; script: Charles Lederer, after a novel by Charles Nordhoff and James Norman Hall; camera: Robert L. Surtees; cast: Marlon Brando (Fletcher Christian), Trevor Howard (William Bligh), Richard Harris (John Mills), Hugh Griffith (Alexander Smith), Taritatumi Teriipaia (Maimiti), and others; length: 179 minutes; production and distribution: Aaron Rosenberg (Arcola)/MGM; première: 1962.

15   THE UGLY AMERICAN
Director: George Englund; script: Stewart Stern, after a novel by William J. Lederer and Eugene Burdick; camera: Clifford Stine; cast: Marlon Brando (Harrison Carter MacWhite), Eiji Okada (Deong), Sandra Church (Marion MacWhite), Pat Hingle (Homer Atkins), Jocelyn Brando (Emma Atkins), and others; length: 120 minutes; Production and distribution: George Englund, Universal Picture; première: 1962.

16   BEDTIME STORY
Director: Ralph Levy; script: Stanley Shapiro and Paul Henning; camera: Clifford Stine; cast: Marlon Brando (Fred Benson), David Niven (Lawrence Jamison), Shirley Jones (Janet Walker), Dody Goodman (Fanny Eubank), and others; length: 99 minutes; production and distribution: Stanley Shapiro (Lankershim-Pennebaker)/Universal Pictures; premiére: 1964.

17   THE SABOTEUR: CODE NAME "MORITUR"
Director: Bernhard Wicki; script: Daniel Taradash, after a novel by Werner Jörg Lüdecke; camera: Conrad Hall; cast: Yul Brynner (captain Müller), Marlon Brando (Robert Crain), Janet Margolin (Esther), Trevor Howard (Colonel Statter), Martin Benrath (Kruse), Hans Christian Blech (Assistent Engineer), Wally Cox (Dr. Ambach), Rainer Penkert (Milkereit), and others; length: 122 minutes; production: Aaron Rosenberg (Arcola-Colony)/Twentieth Century-Fox; première: 1965.

18 THE CHASE
Director: Arthur Penn; script: Lillian Hellman, after a novel by Horton Foote; camera: Joseph La Shelle; cast: Marlon Brando (Sheriff Calder), Jane Fonda (Anna Reeves), Robert Redford (Bubber Reeves), E. G. Marshall (Val Rogers), Angie Dickinson (Ruby Calder), Robert Duvall (Edwin Stewart), Jocelyn Brando (Mrs. Briggs), and others; length: 135 minutes; production: Sam Spiegel (Horizon Picture)/Columbia Pictures; première: 1966.

19 THE APPALOOSA
Director: Sidney J. Furie; script: James Bridges and Roland Kibbee, after a novel by Robert MacLeod; camera: Russell Metty; cast: Marlon Brando (Matt Fletcher), Anjanette Comer (Trini), John Saxon (Chuy Medina), and others; length: 98 minutes; production and distribution: Alan Miller, Universal Pictures; première: 1966.

20 A COUNTESS FROM HONG KONG
Director: Charlie Chaplin; script: Charlie Chaplin; camera: Arthur Ibbetson; cast: Marlon Brando (Ogden Mears), Sophia Loren (Natasha), Sydney Chaplin (Harvey Crothers), Charlie Chaplin (old steward); length: 108 minutes; production and distribution: Jerome Epstein/Universal Pictures; première: 1966 (United Kingdom), 1967 (USA).

21 REFLECTIONS IN A GOLDEN EYE
Director: John Huston; script: Chapman Mortimer and Gladys Hill, after a novel by Carson McCullers; camera: Aldo Tonti; cast: Elizabeth Taylor (Leonora Penderton), Marlon Brando (Major Weldon Penderton), Brian Keith (Morris Langdon), Julie Harris (Alison Langdon), Robert Foster (Williams), and others; length: 109 minutes; production and distribution: Ray Stark/Warner Bros. - Seven Arts; première: 1967.

22 CANDY
Director: Christian Marquand; script: Buck Henry, after a novel by Terry Southern and Mason Hoffenberg; camera: Giuseppe Rotunno; cast: Ewa Aulin (Candy), Charles Aznavour (the hunchback), Marlon Brando (Grindl), Richard Burton (McPhisto), James Coburn (Dr. Krankheit), John Huston (Dr. Dunlap), Walter Matthau (General Smight), Ringo Starr (Emmanuel), and others; length: 123 minutes; production and distribution: Robert Haggiag (Selmur Pictures, Dear Films, Corona)/Cinerama Releasing Corporation; première: 1968.

23 THE NIGHT OF THE FOLLOWING DAY
Director: Hubert Cornfield; script: Hubert Cornfield and Robert Phippeny, after the novel *The Snatchers* by Lionel White; camera: Willi Kurout; cast: Marlon Brando (chauffeur Bud), Richard Boone (Leer), Rita Moreno (Vi), Pamela Franklin (the girl), and others; length: 93 minutes; Production: Hubert Cornfield (Gina)/Universal Release; première: 1969.

24 BURN!
Director: Gillo Pontecorvo; script: Franco Solinas and Giorgio Arlorio; camera: Marcello Gatti; cast: Marlon Brando (Sir William Walker), Evaristo Marquez (José Dolores), Renato Salvatori (Teddy Sanchez), Norman Hill (Shelton), and others; length: 112 minutes; production and distribution: Alberto Grimaldi (Grimaldi, Europee Associates, Les Artistes Associés)/United Artists; première: 1969 (Italy, France).

25 THE NIGHTCOMERS
Director: Michael Winner; script: Michael Hastings, after a short story by Henry James; camera: Robert Paynter; cast: Marlon Brando (Peter Quint), Stephanie Beacham (Margaret Jessel), Thora Hird (Mrs. Grose), Verna Harvey (Flora), Christopher Ellis (Miles), and others; length: 96 minutes; production and distribution: Michael Winner (Elliott Kastner—Jay Kanter—Alan Ladd Jr.—Scimitar)/Avco Embassy; première: 1971 (United Kingdom).

26 THE GODFATHER
Director: Francis Ford Coppola; script: Mario Puzo and Francis Ford Coppola, after the novel by Mario Puzo; camera: Gordon Willis; cast: Marlon Brando (Don Vito Corleone), Al Pacino (Michael Corleone), James Caan (Sonny Corleone), Richard Castellano (Clemenza), Robert Duvall (Tom Hagen), Sterling Hayden (McCluskey), John Marley (Jack Woltz), Diane Keaton (Kay Adams), John Cazale (Fredo Corleone), and others; length: 175 minutes; production and distribution: Albert S. Ruddy/Paramount Pictures; première: 1971.

27 L'ULTIMO TANGO A PARIGI
LE DERNIER TANGO À PARIS
LAST TANGO IN PARIS
Director: Bernardo Bertolucci; script: Bernardo Bertolucci and Franco Arcalli; camera: Vittorio Storaro; cast: Marlon Brando (Paul), Maria Schneider (Jeanne), Jean-Pierre Léaud (Tom), Darling Legitimus (concierge), Massimo Girotti (Marcel), Maria Michi (Rosa's mother), and others; length: 129 minutes; production and distribution: Alberto Grimaldi (PEA, Les Artistes Associés)/United Artists; première: 1972.

28 THE MISSOURI BREAKS
Director: Arthur Penn; script: Thomas McGuane; camera: Michael Butler; cast: Marlon Brando (Robert Lee Clayton), Jack Nicholson (Tom Logan), Randy Quaid (Little Tod), Kathleen

Lloyd (Jane Braxton), and others; length: 126 minutes; production: Robert M. Sherman/United Artists; première: 1976.

29   SUPERMAN
Director: Richard Donner; script: Mario Puzo, David Newman, Robert Benton, Leslie Newman; camera: Geoffrey Unsworth; cast: Christopher Reeve (Superman/Clark Kent), Marlon Brando (Jor El), Gene Hackman (Lex Luthor), Glenn Ford (Pa Kent), and others; length: 143 minutes; production and distribution: Alexander Salkind/Warner Bros.; première: 1978.

30   ROOTS: THE NEW GENERATION
Director: John Erman, Charles S. Dubin, George Stanford Brown, Lloyd Richards; script: Ernest Kinoy, Sidney A. Glass, Thad Mumford, Daniel Wilcox, John McGreevey; camera: Joseph M. Wilcots; cast: among others, Marlon Brando (George Lincoln Rockwell); length: 96 minutes/installment; production: David Wolper, ABC; première: 1979.

31   APOCALYPSE NOW
Director: Francis Ford Coppola; script: John Milius and Francis Ford Coppola, after the novel *Heart of Darkness* by Joseph Conrad; camera: Vittorio Storaro; cast: Marlon Brando (Major Kurtz), Robert Duvall (Major Kilgore), Martin Sheen (Captain Willard), Frederic Forrest ("Boss"), Dennis Hopper (photographer), and others; length: 153 minutes; production and distribution: Omni Zoetrope/United Artists; première: 1979.

32   THE FORMULA
Director: John G. Avildsen; script: Steven Shagan, after his novel; camera: James Crabe; cast: George C. Scott (Barney Caine), Marlon Brando (Adam Steiffel), Marthe Keller (Lisa), John Gielgud (Dr. Esau), and others; length: 117 minutes; production and distribution: Steven Shagan, MGM; première: 1980.

33   A DRY WHITE SEASON
Director: Euzhan Palcy; script: Collin Welland and Euzhan Palcy, after a novel by André Brink; camera: Kevin Pike and Pierre-William Glenn; cast: Donald Sutherland (Ben), Janet Suzman (Susan), Zakes Mokae (Stanley), Jürgen Prochnow (Captain Stolz), Susan Sarandon (Melanie), Marlon Brando (Ian McKenzie), and others; length: 107 minutes; production and distribution: MGM; première: 1989.

34   THE FRESHMAN
Director: Andrew Bergman; script: Andrew Bergman; camera: William A. Fraker; cast: Marlon Brando (Carmine Sabatini), Matthew Broderick (Clark Kellog), Bruno Kirby (Victor Ray), Penelope Ann Miller (Tina Sabatini), Frank Whaley (Steve Bushak), and others; length: 102 minutes; production and distribution: Lobell Bergman/Tri-Star; première: 1990.

35   CHRISTOPHER COLUMBUS — THE DISCOVERY
Director: John Glen; script: John Briley, Cary Bates, Mario Puzo; camera: Alec Mills; cast: Georges Corraface (Christopher Columbus), Tom Selleck (King Fernando of Aragon), Rachel Ward (Queen Isabella), Marlon Brando (Tomas de Torquemada), Mathieu Carrière (King John) and others; length: 121 minutes; production and distribution: Alexander & Ilya Salkind/Scotia, Constantin, Monopole Pathé; première: 1990.

36   DON JUAN DeMARCO
Director: Jeremy Leven; script: Jeremy Leven; camera: Ralf Bode; cast: Marlon Brando (Dr. Jack Mickler), Johnny Depp (Don Juan DeMarco), Faye Dunaway (Marilyn Mickler), Geraldine Pailhas (Doña Inez), and others; length: 94 minutes; production and distribution: Francis Ford Coppola, Fred Fuchs, Patrick Palmer (American Zoetrope)/New Line; première: 1995.